# BOSWORTH 1485

# BOSWORTH 1485

MIKE INGRAM

First published by Spellmount, an imprint of The History Press, 2012





Printed in India

North American edition published by Dundurn Press, 2016



ISBN 978 1 4597 3396 1
A Cataloguing-in-Publication record for this book is available from Library and Archives Canada.

This book is also available in electronic formats: ISBN 978 1 4597 3397 8 (pdf); ISBN 978 1 4597 3398 5 (e-pub).



Visit us at
Dundurn.com | @dundurnpress | Facebook.com/dundurnpress
Pinterest/dundurnpress

Dundurn
3 Church Street, Suite 500
Toronto, Ontario, Canada
M5E 1M2

# CONTENTS

# ACKNOWLEDGEMENTS

Firstly, I must thank Jo de Vries, series editor, for her suggestion that I should write this book in the first place and for her guidance.

Special thanks must go to Ian Post for his support over the years, his suggestions, and our many, often long discussions on how events unfolded in 1485. The same must go to Joe Ann Ricca of the Richard III Foundation for her interest in the project, her suggestions and support. I must also thank Toby McLeod for his words of wisdom, Richard Mackinder at the Bosworth Battlefield Centre, Allan Harley and the members of the Beaufort Household and Medieval Siege Society who helped with the practicalities of medieval warfare. I must also thank all those, too many to mention by name, who were involved in finding the actual site of the battle, and making this book possible.

The last words, however, must go to my children, Finley and Ellen – this book is for you.

# LIST OF ILLUSTRATIONS

## Maps

# INTRODUCTION

A horse! A horse! My kingdom for a horse!
William Shakespeare, *Richard III*, Act V, Scene VII

These are the famous last words of Richard III at the Battle of Bosworth, at least according to William Shakespeare. Shakespeare's version of events and the image that the last Plantagenet King of England was a misshapen antichrist have always clouded the truth of Richard III's life. Since then, there have been many tomes written by both the supporters and detractors of Richard III; of the mysterious death of the Princes in the Tower; and of the usurpation of the throne itself. Indeed, scholars and historians will no doubt continue to debate Richard's character and life for many years to come.

This book, however, is not about a king, but about one of, if not the, most important battle in English history after the Battle of Hastings in 1066. The Battle of Bosworth (or Redemoor) was fought on 22 August 1485 and was the penultimate battle of the Wars of the Roses, a series of dynastic civil wars fought for the throne of England. It is often regarded as the end of the Middle Ages and the beginning of the Renaissance, although in reality the change was much more gradual. Nevertheless, it does mark the beginning of the reign of the Tudors, with Henry VII taking the throne at the end of this fateful day, before his son Henry VIII and his granddaughter Elizabeth I would go on to lead the country to previously unknown greatness.

Considering its importance, very little was written about the battle either at the time or during Henry's reign. Not only that, but most accounts were written by people with either little or no concern for military tactics, making any reconstruction of the battle difficult. It would be another 160 years and another important battle in English history, Naseby, before the tactics and dispositions of the troops would be recorded in any detail. It is also an old adage that history is written by the victor, but in the medieval period it usually was, and as such was heavily biased.

Of all the accounts, the *Crowland Chronicle* is probably the most contemporary. It was commissioned by the Benedictine Abbey of Crowland (or Croyland) in Lincolnshire and was written in two parts known as the First and Second Continuations. The Second Continuation, which details the battle and the events leading up to it, was probably written the year after the event. Its author was most likely John Russell, Bishop of Lincoln, who was keeper of the privy seal for Edward IV and chancellor under Richard III. He probably accompanied Richard III on the campaign and as such was well informed. However, he was not an eyewitness to the battle and does little to disguise his dislike of Richard's rule.

Polydore Vergil was an Italian who came to England in 1502 as a deputy to the collector of papal taxes, Cardinal Adriano Castelli. He wrote his description of the battle in his *Historiae Anglicae* between 1503 and 1513, probably at the request of Henry VII. Unusually for the time, he gives a detailed description of events during the battle, no doubt using eyewitness testimony. Vergil himself says that his account is truthful and, considering he had no allegiance to either party, is probably correct. Both the Tudor chroniclers Hall and Holinshed made use of it, and later Shakespeare would use these two texts to write his history of Richard III. Another source for the battle is Jean Molinet's *Chroniques*. Molinet, who was the historian to the Burgundian court and sympathetic to the Yorkist cause, wrote his account of Bosworth in around 1504, probably based on stories told by French troops and in the court.

Burgundian nobleman Philippe de Commines (or Commynes) wrote his eight-volume *Memoirs* during the 1490s, although as he was one of Louis XI of France's most trusted advisors, his account of the battle and the events leading up to it are biased towards Henry Tudor and his supporters. Although well written, his account has to be treated with caution because his information would have been based on rumour and second- or third-hand accounts, and it also appears that in parts he was guilty of altering events to suit his own ends. A further foreign account was written for the Spanish king and queen, Ferdinand and Isabella, in March 1486 by Diego de Valera, a Castilian courtier, but much of his information appears to come from Spanish merchants returning from England and is confused in places. There are a number of other sources such as *Historia Johannis Rossi Warwicensis de Regibus Anglie* written by John Rous (*c.* 1490); *The Chronicle of Fabian* by Robert Fabian (*c.* 1510); and the *Pittscottie's Chronicles* by Robert Lindsay of Pittscottie (*c.* 1570). All these works mention the battle in passing, but give little detail. Edward Hall, a London lawyer, also wrote *The Union of the Two Noble Families of Lancaster and York* in around 1550, which primarily follows Vergil's work and includes other parts from de Commines, Fabian and other now obscure sources. Throughout his work Hall includes lengthy speeches, no doubt dramatic invention, and it is likely that Shakespeare derived some of his history from here.

Probably written early in the sixteenth century, *The Ballad of Bosworth Field* gives a poetic account of the battle in over 600 lines. It was commissioned by a member of the Stanley family, with Lord Thomas and Sir William Stanley playing a central role.

Its accuracy has long been debated, although it does contain information collaborated by other sources as well as detail not found anywhere else. The same anonymous author probably wrote two other ballads, *The Song of Lady Bessy* and *The Rose of England*, both including accounts of the battle with a strong bias towards the Stanleys. Again they contain information found elsewhere, but like *The Ballad of Bosworth Field* are considered suspect by some historians. Another poetic account of the battle was written by Baronet, Sir John Beaumont around 1600 and is called *Bosworth Field*. Beaumont studied at Broadgate's Hall (now Pembroke College), Oxford, and lived at Thringstone, not far from the battlefield. He was a descendant of both William Hastings, who was controversially executed by Richard III, and the earls of Oxford, whilst his father was a judge of the Common Pleas. It is written in the style of the heroic poems of old and much of what he wrote is found in other sources such as Hall, although there are a few interesting sections that go into extraordinary detail and are not recorded anywhere else.

For many years the location of the battle was thought to be on Ambion Hill, close to the village of Sutton Cheney in Leicestershire. In 2010, after a major archaeological project, the actual site of the battle was announced to the public as being 3km from Ambion Hill, close to Fenn Lane. Although the site of the famous battle is now known, there are still many more unanswered questions: the dispositions of the three armies; their locations before and during the battle; the location of the artillery; and how events unfolded that day. All of these questions are open to a number of interpretations due to the scarcity and ambiguities of the sources.

Battles are notoriously difficult to interpret and we still do not know exactly what happened during many of the battles of the First World War, even with the huge amounts of documentation and plentiful eyewitness testimony available. So for the medieval period it is almost impossible to say what happened with any degree of certainty. The Battle of Bosworth is a prime example and, until very recently, events have all been based on Ambion Hill, with more than one historian making the events fit the site. This book is therefore just one interpretation of that day and there will no doubt be others – until someone invents a time machine the truth will probably never be known.

# TIMELINE

| | | |
|---|---|---|
| 1411 | 22 September | Birth of Richard Plantagenet, future Duke of York |
| 1413 | 20 March | Death of Henry IV; uncontested accession of Henry V |
| 1415 | 25 October | Battle of Agincourt – Henry V wins major victory over the French |
| 1420 | 22 May | Treaty of Troyes recognises Henry V as heir to Charles VI of France |
| | 2 June | Henry V marries Catherine of Valois, daughter of Charles VI of France |
| 1421 | 6 December | Prince Henry, son of Henry V and future Henry VI, is born at Windsor |
| 1422 | 31 August | Death of Henry V; accession of 9-month-old Henry VI |
| | 6 November | Henry VI is crowned King of England at Westminster |
| 1442 | 28 April | Birth of Edward, Earl of March, eldest son of the Duke of York and future Edward IV |
| 1445 | 23 April | Henry VI marries Margaret of Anjou |
| 1449 | 21 October | Birth of George, son of the Duke of York, and future Duke of Clarence |
| | 29 October | English surrender Rouen, the capital of Normandy, to the French |

| | | |
|---|---|---|
| 1450 | June–July | Jack Cade's rebels occupy London |
| | 12 August | The French capture Cherbourg and end English rule in Normandy |
| 1452 | 2 October | Birth of Richard, youngest son of the Duke of York and future Richard III |
| 1453 | 17 July | French victory at Castillon ends English rule in Gascony |
| | c. 1 August | Onset of Henry VI's first bout of mental illness |
| | 13 October | Birth of Edward of Lancaster, son of Henry VI and Margaret of Anjou |
| 1454 | 27 March | York is named Lord Protector during the king's illness |
| | c. 25 December | Henry VI recovers from mental illness |
| 1455 | January | York surrenders the office of protector |
| | 22 May | First Battle of St Albans – York and his allies, the Neville earls of Salisbury and Warwick, win control of the king and kill their chief enemies: Somerset, Northumberland and Clifford |
| | 19 November | York is appointed Lord Protector for the second time |
| 1457 | 28 January | Birth of Henry Tudor, Earl of Richmond, the future Henry VII |
| 1459 | 23 September | Battle of Blore Heath – Richard Neville, Earl of Salisbury, defeats a Lancastrian force trying to block his junction with York |
| | 12–13 October | Heavily outnumbered, the Yorkist lords flee from Ludford Bridge; York goes to Ireland; Warwick, Salisbury and March go to Calais |
| 1460 | 26 June | Yorkist earls of Warwick, Salisbury and March land in England from Calais |
| | 10 July | Battle of Northampton – Warwick captures Henry VI and control of the government |

| | | |
|---|---|---|
| | **30 December** | Battle of Wakefield – defeat and death of York and Salisbury, and York's second son, Edmund Plantagenet, Earl of Rutland |
| 1461 | **2 February** | Battle of Mortimer's Cross – Yorkist victory in Wales |
| | **17 February** | Second Battle of St Albans – Margaret of Anjou defeats Warwick and reunites herself and her son with Henry VI |
| | **4 March** | Edward, Earl of March, is proclaimed King Edward IV at Westminster |
| | **27–28 March** | Battle of Ferrybridge – Lancastrian attempts to prevent a Yorkist crossing of the River Aire |
| | **29 March** | Battle of Towton – Edward IV wins throne and Henry VI and his family flee into Scotland |
| | **28 June** | Official coronation of Edward IV |
| 1464 | **1 May** | Edward IV secretly marries Elizabeth Woodville |
| | **25 December** | Elizabeth Woodville is publicly introduced to the court as queen |
| 1465 | **13 July** | Henry VI is captured in Lancashire and imprisoned in the Tower of London |
| 1469 | **April–July** | Robin of Redesdale's rebellion is fomented by Warwick |
| | **26 July** | Battle of Edgecote Moor – a royal army led by William Herbert, Earl of Pembroke, is beaten by Warwick's rebels |
| 1470 | **12 March** | Battle of Losecote Field – Edward IV defeats rebels operating under the direction of Warwick and Clarence |
| | **2 November** | Birth of Prince Edward, eldest son of Edward IV, future Edward V |
| 1471 | **14 April** | Battle of Barnet – Warwick is defeated and killed; Margaret of Anjou lands at Weymouth |

| | | |
|---|---|---|
| | **4 May** | Battle of Tewkesbury – Prince Edward of Lancaster is killed |
| | **7 May** | Margaret of Anjou is captured and taken to the Tower of London |
| | **21 May** | Edward IV enters London in triumph; Henry VI is murdered in the Tower of London |
| | **2 June** | Jasper Tudor, Earl of Pembroke, escapes from England with his nephew, Henry Tudor, Earl of Richmond |
| 1473 | ***c*. 17 August** | Birth of Richard, second son of Edward IV, future Duke of York |
| 1478 | **18 February** | George, Duke of Clarence, is executed in the Tower of London |
| 1483 | **9 April** | Death of Edward IV; accession of Edward V |
| | **30 April** | Richard, Duke of Gloucester, takes charge of his nephew, Edward V, at Stony Stratford on the road to London |
| | **22 June** | Dr Ralph Shaa delivers a public sermon at Paul's Cross in London setting forth Richard of Gloucester's claim to the throne |
| | **26 June** | Henry Stafford, Duke of Buckingham, presents Richard of Gloucester with a petition requesting him to take the throne |
| | **6 July** | Richard of Gloucester is crowned Richard III in Westminster Abbey |
| | **25 December** | Henry Tudor, Earl of Richmond, takes oath to marry Elizabeth of York, eldest daughter of Edward IV |
| 1484 | **23 January** | Richard III's only Parliament opens at Westminster; *Titulus Regius* is passed |
| | **April** | Death of Edward of Middleham, only child of Richard III |
| | **September** | Henry Tudor, Earl of Richmond, flees from Brittany to France |

| | | |
|---|---|---|
| 1485 | **7 August** | Henry Tudor, Earl of Richmond, lands with an invasion force at Milford Haven in Wales |
| | **22 August** | Battle of Bosworth Field – Richard III is defeated and killed; accession of Henry Tudor, Earl of Richmond, as Henry VII |
| | **30 October** | Coronation of Henry VII |
| | **7 November** | Henry VII's first Parliament opens at Westminster |
| 1486 | **18 January** | Henry VII marries Elizabeth of York, daughter of Edward IV |
| | **19 September** | Birth of Prince Arthur, first child of Henry VII |
| 1487 | **24 May** | Lambert Simnel, who claims to be a nephew of Edward IV, is crowned King of England in Dublin |
| | **16 June** | Battle of Stoke – Henry VII defeats Yorkist supporters of Lambert Simnel |
| 1491 | **28 June** | Birth of Prince Henry, future Henry VIII |

# HISTORICAL BACKGROUND

Ye shall hear of wars and rumours of war;
see that ye be not troubled, for all these things
must come to pass, but the end is not yet.

Matthew 26:6

The Wars of the Roses were like no other in the medieval world as they were neither for for land, wealth nor religious ideals, but the right to rule the country. For the majority of the time it was relatively peaceful, with most of the 'war' being fought with words and political manoeuvring within the royal court. In fact, there were only sixteen major battles and half of these occurred between 1460 and 1465. The wars began with Jack Cade's rebellion against Henry VI in 1450 and lasted thirty-seven years, but rather than one long war it was a series of interconnected campaigns in five distinct phases.

## A Family Divided

The wars may have started in 1450, but we have to go back a hundred years to the reign of Edward III to find its roots. Edward III, unlike his father Edward II, was a strong and energetic king, who

## The Wars of the Roses

Sir Walter Scott is usually credited with coining the term 'Wars of the Roses' in his 1829 novel *Anne of Geierstein*. Before then, the wars were generally known as the 'Cousin's Wars'. Whilst the white rose was one of the badges of the House of York, the red rose was not used as a badge of the House of Lancaster until Henry Tudor was on the throne.

succeeded in regaining royal authority and transforming England into one of the most formidable military powers in Europe. In 1337, and after Edward declared himself rightful heir to the French throne, conflict with the French was inevitable and the series of wars that followed, known as the Hundred Years War, ravaged France and the south coast of England until 1453. Within a few years, England controlled huge parts of France, prompting the contemporary chronicler Jean Froissart to write of Edward, 'His like had not been seen since the days of King Arthur'.

To prosecute a war of this scale, Edward needed huge amounts of manpower, but soon found that the old feudal system of obligatory service was ineffective. Instead, he created a system of recruitment by contract, with the nobles acting as recruitment agents: the nobles recruited lesser nobles, who in turn would each recruit a set number of men or even lesser nobles and so on. In return for a fixed period in the army, a soldier could expect to receive pay, clothing and support from the noble, and all this would be laid out in a written contract. In effect, this created private armies for the nobles. Under a strong king and a common cause this system was very effective; however, as we shall see, in different circumstances it was also open to abuse.

Edward had five sons who were to reach maturity: Edward of Woodstock, Prince of Wales (the name Black Prince came long after his death); Lionel of Antwerp, 1st Duke of Clarence; John of Gaunt, 1st Duke of Lancaster; Edmund of Langley, 1st Duke of York; and Thomas of Woodstock, 1st Duke of Gloucester. Edward, as the eldest, was heir to the throne and appeared to be following in his father's footsteps after the stunning victories over the French at Crécy and Poitiers. However, tragedy struck in 1376 when he died after an illness. Edward III died a year later and in accordance with the rules of succession, the Black Prince's 10-year-old son Richard succeeded to the throne.

Richard II's reign was a troubled one, and plots and revolts continually plagued him. He did not enjoy war as his father and grandfather had done and negotiated a twenty-eight-year truce with the French, losing much of the past won territories in the process. As the years passed, Richard became more tyrannical, possibly due to some form of mental illness. As he had not produced an heir, Richard named his cousin Roger Mortimer, 4th Earl of March, as his successor. The earls of March (the March was the borderlands between England and Wales) were the chief Anglo-Norman lords in Ireland and the second most senior line of descent in succession to the throne through Roger's mother Phillipa, only daughter of Lionel of Antwerp.

Next in the line of succession was Richard's uncle, John of Gaunt, Duke of Lancaster. During Richard's minority, Gaunt had effectively ruled the country and had become the wealthiest and most powerful man in England after the king. He also had an eye for the ladies, marrying three times. His third wife was his long-time mistress Katherine Swynford and they already had three sons by the time they were married and legitimised by Parliament in 1397. The children took the family name of Beaufort and were eventually known as the dukes of Somerset.

On Gaunt's death in 1399, Richard II confiscated all his land and exiled his son and heir, Henry of Bolingbroke, for life. Wishing to reclaim his lands, Henry returned to England with an army, and on a tide of popular support, aided by disaffected nobles, he was soon in control of the kingdom. On 13 October 1399 he was proclaimed King Henry IV, bypassing the descendants of Edward III's second surviving son, Lionel of Antwerp, 1st Duke of Clarence. Meanwhile, Richard II was held captive in Pontefract Castle where he eventually died, probably from starvation, in February 1400. The House of Lancaster now ruled over England.

Henry IV's reign, like Richard II's before him, was plagued by rebellion, which was often instigated in part by the Mortimers, rightful heirs to the throne, and Henry Percy, Earl of Northumberland, with his son, Harry Hotspur. However, Henry IV survived and in 1413 his son Henry V peacefully succeeded him.

Henry V was the epitome of medieval kingship and an outstanding military commander. He renewed the war against France with vigour and his famous victory at the Battle of Agincourt has long since entered national myth. Henry conquered much of northern France, which resulted in the signing of the Treaty of Troyes in 1420, recognising Henry as the heir to the French Crown. His successes intensified English pride in the king and his dynasty, ending the uprisings that marked his early reign. He also married Catherine of Valois, the daughter of Charles VI of France, which further strengthened his claim to the French throne.

In 1402 Edward III's last surviving son, Edmund of Langley, 1st Duke of York, died at the age of 61. Although a competent military commander during the Hundred Years War, he was retiring and unambitious, playing little part in the politics of the time. Edmund's eldest son, Edward, inherited the dukedom but was killed at Agincourt without an heir, while his younger son, Richard, had married his cousin twice-removed, Anne Mortimer. The same year as his brother was killed in battle, Richard was executed following his involvement in the Southampton plot to depose Henry in favour of the Earl of March. The dukedom of York therefore passed to his son, another Richard, who was just 4 years old. Through his mother, Richard junior also inherited the lands of the earldom of March, as well as the Mortimer claim to the throne; the House of York was finally going to step into the limelight.

Tragedy struck in August 1422 when Henry V died, probably from dysentery, and once again the country found itself ruled by a child – the 1-year-old son of Henry V. During the king's minority, the longest in English history, England was governed by a council that included the king's younger uncle, Humphrey, Duke of Gloucester, and his great-uncle, Henry Beaufort, Bishop of Winchester. English territories in France, which by this time amounted to almost a third of the country, were governed by Henry's eldest paternal uncle, John, Duke of Bedford. Henry VI was crowned at Westminster in 1429 and under the terms of the Treaty of Troyes was to be proclaimed King of France on the death of Charles VI. However, in 1429 the peace that had followed the treaty was shattered when, with the help of Joan of Arc, Charles VI's son was crowned King Charles VII in Reims.

In 1437, 15-year-old Henry was declared old enough to rule England, but unfortunately he lacked the charisma and strength of his father, with Pope Pius II describing him as 'a man more timorous than a woman, utterly devoid of wit or spirit'. Henry was an exceptionally pious man, with no interest in war, and spent his time on pursuits such as the foundation of Eton College and King's College, Cambridge, to which he diverted funds that were urgently needed elsewhere. He had little understanding of the workings of government and much of the day-to-day running of the country was carried out by the royal council. These were advisors selected by the king to give counsel on questions of foreign and domestic policy, as well as raising finance, dispensing justice and conducting the daily administration of the country. Unsurprisingly, the great nobles considered themselves his natural advisors and the weak-willed Henry was easily persuaded by the self-interested nobles and frequently granted titles, lands, offices, pardons and monetary rewards without any thought to the merits or the consequences of their requests.

One of these nobles was Richard, Duke of York, who at the age of 18 married Cecily Neville, daughter of the Earl of Westmorland

and sister of Richard Neville, the powerful Earl of Salisbury. By 1430 he was constable of England, and two years later appointed Guardian of the Coast of Normandy. In 1436 he was appointed to the most prestigious post in the royal court, the king's lieutenant in France, although due to the poor state of the royal finances, largely due to Henry's spending (in one year alone he spent the entire royal income on his court), York financed most of his campaigns himself.

Preferring to pursue a policy of peace between the two countries, Henry allowed England's military position in France to deteriorate. In 1444 a truce was negotiated with France and marriage was arranged between the 23-year-old Henry and Charles' 16-year-old niece, Margaret of Anjou. Once crowned, it would not take long for the formidable Margaret to establish herself as the power behind the throne and, like her husband, had her favourites in court. Henry, anxious to achieve a final settlement in France, soon fulfilled a rash promise to surrender Maine and Anjou in western France, but the decision to sue for peace was not popular with the English people or the Duke of York, who openly opposed it in court. This led to York being replaced in France by one of Henry's favourites, his cousin Edmund Beaufort, Duke of Somerset, in 1446. To add insult to injury, York was made lieutenant of Ireland for the next ten years, effectively sending him into exile.

In 1449 war with France flared up again; however, the Duke of Somerset was a poor military commander and was responsible for the surrender of the strategic town of Rouen, the gateway to Normandy, and within a year Normandy itself had fallen. As a consequence, Somerset became distinctly unpopular and although he retained the king's favour, maintaining his prestigious position at court, his continuing presence fuelled unrest at home.

The recruitment of troops under contract instigated by Edward III had grown into a system of 'Livery and Maintenance', which maintained the feudalism of the previous years and is

## Fifteenth-century England

The population of England in the fifteenth century was around 2.5 million people, i.e. about the same as modern-day Greater Manchester in England, Brooklyn in the United States or Toronto in Canada. It was primarily a rural economy, with wool and cloth being the main products, and 80 per cent of the population were employed in agriculture and living in the countryside.

referred to as 'bastard feudalism' by some historians. Livery, an expression deriving from the French word *livrée,* meaning delivered, referred to the badge or emblem in the lord's colours, given to a retainer (employee). Maintenance referred to the lord's duty to maintain or support his retainers, by word or action, in any lawsuit in which they were involved. By the fifteenth century, maintenance, although banned by law, had become one of the recognised benefits of 'good lordship' that a retainer could expect from the magnate to whom he had sworn allegiance. During the 1440s and 1450s, as the influence and authority of the Crown declined, maintenance began to have a far more sinister meaning – the bribing, intimidating, or even kidnapping of judges, jurors, witnesses and opposing councillors. The country was, in effect, being run by the medieval version of the mafia.

## Descent into War

In June 1450, 3,000 men of Kent and Sussex rose in revolt and marched on London, led by a mysterious figure known as Jack Cade. Unlike the Peasants' Revolt almost seventy years earlier, their number included lords, landowners and merchants. Their demands were simple: the removal from power of those they considered traitors (such as Somerset); the restoration of

## English towns

Of all the towns and cities in England, only thirty had an estimated population greater than 2,000: London was the biggest with around 40,000 inhabitants; York was the next largest with 12,000 people; followed by Bristol (10,600); and Coventry (8,000). Leicester and Nottingham, both important residences of Richard III during the 1485 crisis, only had populations of 3,500 and 2,500 respectively.

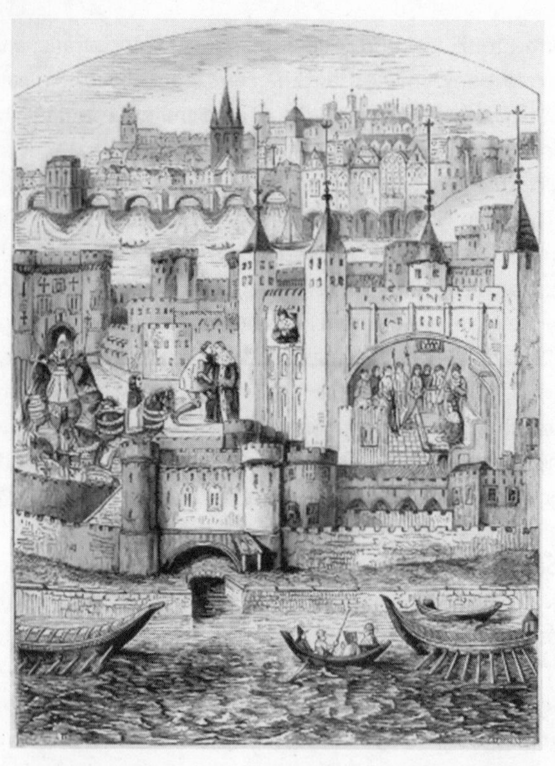

*1. London from a fifteenth-century manuscript. (Author's collection)*

justice to the counties; and the placing of men of royal blood (such as York) in key positions. As with so many other protests of this type, it began peacefully but soon turned ugly. After presenting their complaints, the rebels began to return home; however, the king's men began to harry the rebels and attacked the county of Kent as well, threatening to turn it into a 'deer forest'. The rebels returned to London, dragging members of Henry's council into the street and executing them. An orgy of violence and looting followed and only ended when the citizens of London drove them out after vicious street fighting which left hundreds dead.

Within weeks, York returned to England without permission, and after evading an attempt by Henry to intercept him, arrived in London on 27 September. By this time, the unrest in London was such that Somerset had to be put in the Tower of London for his own safety. In April 1451 Somerset was released from the Tower and appointed captain of Calais. When one of York's councillors, Thomas Young, the MP for Bristol, proposed that York be recognised as heir to the throne, he was sent to the Tower and Parliament was dissolved. Frustrated by his lack of political power, York retired to Ludlow. In 1452, York, declaring that his sole object was to get rid of Henry of Somerset and other evil councillors, raised a force and marched on London. Henry and a royal army met him at Dartford and York laid before him a bill of accusation against Somerset, before swearing fealty to the king. However, York still lacked any real support outside Parliament and his own retainers. Later, a bitter feud between the Neville and Percy families boiled over into armed conflict, with Somerset supporting the Percys' cause. The Nevilles, although related to York, had up to this point been Lancastrian supporters, but with Somerset against them they sided with York.

During the summer of 1453 everything changed. Firstly, Margaret of Anjou found herself pregnant. Then, in August an attempt to regain lost territory in France ended in disaster when

## Calais

An English possession since 1347, the French Channel town of Calais was of immense military importance during the Wars of the Roses. It consisted of the port itself, around 32km (20 miles) of coast, extending 9km (6 miles) inland. It was ringed with castles and had a population of around 5,000, including 1,000 soldiers.

an English army in Gascony was ripped to shreds by French artillery at the Battle of Castillon, the defeat spelling the end of English rule in France. Soon after, Henry VI suffered a catastrophic mental breakdown, becoming completely unresponsive and having to be led from room to room. Modern analysis of his symptoms have led experts to agree that it was a form of schizophrenia, probably inherited from his grandfather, Charles VI of France, who believed he was made of glass. With no sign of Henry recovering, a Great Council was called, and despite attempts by Somerset to prevent him attending and protestations by Margaret of Anjou, York was appointed Protector of the Realm and chief councillor.

York wasted no time in committing Somerset to the Tower and appointing his brother-in-law, Richard Neville, 5th Earl of Salisbury, as chancellor. When Henry recovered his reason in January 1455, York was quickly dismissed and Somerset released. York, Salisbury and Salisbury's eldest son, Richard Neville, Earl of Warwick (who would be known to future generations as 'the Kingmaker'), returned to their estates and gathered their armies; York's dispute with Somerset would have to be settled by force. On one side was the House of York, with their powerful Neville supporters, and on the other was the House of Lancaster, supported by Somerset and the Percy family, earls of Northumberland.

Whilst the two sides were squaring up to each other, a marriage took place that would have far-reaching effects on the future of

England. It was the marriage of Edmund Tudor, Earl of Richmond, to 12-year-old Margaret Beaufort, great-granddaughter of John of Gaunt. Tudor was the half-brother of Henry, the eldest son of a secret marriage between his mother, Catherine of Valois, and a Welshman named Owen Tudor, one of her household servants. Their son Henry was born the following year and would give the Lancastrians an alternative, although tentative, line of succession to the throne.

On 21 April, the king and his advisors decided to hold a council at Leicester the following month. York, Salisbury and Warwick were invited of course, but they suspected it was a trap and instead decided to intercept the king and take him into their 'protection'. The two sides collided at St Albans on 22 May, although the fighting that followed was closer to an armed brawl than a battle. However, significantly, among the dead was Somerset, Henry Percy, 2nd Earl of Northumberland, and Thomas Clifford, 8th Baron de Clifford, plus the king was effectively York's prisoner.

King Henry once again went into decline and York was again made protector. His protectorate lasted until February the next year when the king began to recover. With the birth of her son, Margaret of Anjou began to get more involved with the affairs of state and court politics, removing Yorkist sympathisers from positions of royal office, including Warwick, who was now captain of Calais, by starving him of funds in an attempt to force him out. However, Warwick turned to what was effectively piracy to pay his troops and continued in his position. With all attempts to stop York and his supporters ending in failure, Margaret played her last card in June 1459 by charging the Yorkists with treason. In response, York began to gather his forces at Ludlow Castle. Salisbury, en route to join up with the gathering Yorkist army, was intercepted by an army under Lord Audley at Blore Heath. In the battle that followed, the Lancastrians were beaten and Audley killed during a massed cavalry charge.

## The War of Succession

The royal army, now under the command of the queen's new favourite, Henry Stafford, Duke of Buckingham and a great-grandson of Edward III through Thomas of Woodstock, marched on Ludlow. However, York was ready and formed a defensive position at Ludford Bridge, but disaster struck when Andrew Trollop and a contingent of men from Calais defected to the king's cause. York and Edmund, his eldest son, were forced to flee to Ireland, while Warwick and Edward, York's second son, marched to Calais. In 1460, the Yorkist lords planned a return to England.

The Calais lords, as they were known, landed at Sandwich in Kent and marched north, while the Lancastrians, who were now based at Coventry, marched south to meet them. The two sides clashed at Northampton on 10 July 1460. Mid-battle, Lord Grey came over to the Yorkist side and in the ensuing battle all the Lancastrian commanders were killed and the king taken into custody. York returned soon after and for the first time asserted his claim to the throne. After a long discussion a compromise was effected, by which Henry was to retain the Crown during his lifetime, after which it was to revert to York and his heirs.

However, Margaret, who refused to recognise this arrangement, had been collecting an army in the north. The two sides clashed again at Wakefield on 30 December 1460, but this time both York and his eldest son were killed. Richard's claim to the throne was then passed to his son Edward, who went on to defeat the Lancastrians at Mortimer's Cross on 2 February 1461. However, the tables were turned when Warwick was defeated by a Lancastrian army at the Second Battle of St Albans on 17 March, although, despite this setback, Edward was formally declared king in London on 4 March 1461. Edward and Warwick then went on to virtually wipe out the Lancastrian army at the Battle of Towton twenty-five days later, which is still known today as the bloodiest battle on English soil with a reported 28,000 deaths on the battlefield.

The early reign of Edward IV was marred by Lancastrian plotting and uprisings in favour of Henry VI. On 1 May 1464, Edward secretly married Elizabeth Woodville (or Wydeville), the daughter of Richard Woodville, Lord Rivers, and Jacquetta of Luxembourg, Duchess of Bedford, after a whirlwind romance. It was the first royal match with an Englishwoman since the thirteenth century and was immediately unpopular. Elizabeth was a strong-willed woman and brought her large, ambitious family to court and they were soon occupying key government positions, which alienated Warwick and Richard, Duke of Gloucester.

## The Destruction of the Nevilles and Lancaster

In 1469, Warwick, with his influence in court waning, instigated a rebellion. An army led by 'Robin of Redesdale' marching south was met by a largely Welsh army sent by Edward to suppress them at Edgecote on 26 July. The ensuing battle was a disaster for the Yorkists and the flower of Welsh nobility was either cut down or executed. Edward himself was taken prisoner soon after, and the senior Woodvilles, Earl Rivers and Sir John Woodville, were captured and executed. However, with the political tide still against him, Warwick was forced to release Edward in October. The following year Warwick tried again, this time siding with Edward's jealous brother George, Duke of Clarence, and Margaret of Anjou, who had been in exile in France for nine years. In September 1470, Edward was once again forced to flee the country with his youngest brother Richard, Duke of Gloucester. The Kingmaker wasted no time in putting Henry VI back on the throne, declaring Edward illegitimate and therefore not entitled to rule.

It was to be a short reign, for on 14 March the following year Edward returned with an army. He first marched to York and then to Coventry, and was heading for London when he found the way barred by Warwick's army at Barnet on 14 April. It was to be Warwick's last battle and the 18-year-old Richard of Gloucester's first. The thick morning fog hampered both sides, but eventually Warwick's troops were routed and Warwick himself was cut down trying to make his escape. Edward was once again king and Henry was made a prisoner in the Tower of London.

As Edward's army was battling Warwick's, a new threat appeared when Margaret of Anjou landed at Weymouth with another army. Margaret headed for the Welsh border regions so she could join with Jasper Tudor, Earl of Pembroke, who was another of Henry's half-brothers. Edward marched to meet them and the two sides fought at Tewkesbury on 4 May. It was a

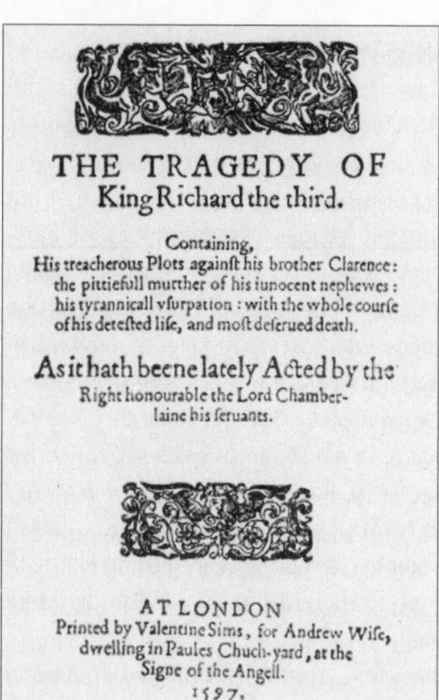

THE TRAGEDY OF
King Richard the third.

Containing,
His treacherous Plots against his brother Clarence:
the pittiefull murther of his iunocent nephewes:
his tyrannicall vsurpation: with the whole course
of his detested life, and most deserued death.

As it hath beene lately Acted by the
Right honourable the Lord Chamber-
laine his seruants.

AT LONDON
Printed by Valentine Sims, for Andrew Wise,
dwelling in Paules Chuch-yard, at the
Signe of the Angell.
1597.

*2. One of the earliest published copies of Shakespeare's play* Richard III. *His version of events has clouded the history ever since. (Author's collection)*

decisive victory for the Yorkists, with the last of the Lancastrians, including Margaret's son, the 17-year-old Prince Edward, killed or executed. The handful of Lancastrian supporters that remained escaped to France, including Jasper Tudor and his young nephew, Henry. By the end of the month Henry VI was also dead, with the circumstances of his death shrouded in mystery. It was the end of the struggle between the Houses of York and Lancaster, or so it was thought.

The next twelve years passed relatively peacefully, with the only notable exception being the arrest of Edward IV's brother George, Duke of Clarence, in June 1477. Clarence was charged with treason in the following January and executed. Tradition says he was executed by drowning in a barrel of Malmsey wine (claret), although the exact method of his execution is uncertain.

## The Usurpation of the Throne

On 9 April 1483, Edward died unexpectedly, just before his forty-first birthday. The crown passed to his 12-year-old son, Prince Edward, who was recognised as Edward V and escorted to London by his Woodville relatives, including Earl Rivers. However, Richard and his close advisor Henry Stafford, Duke of Buckingham and a descendant of Edward III through Thomas of Woodstock, intercepted the royal party at Stony Stratford, arrested Rivers, took custody of the king and escorted him to the Bishop of London's palace.

On 30 April, the queen and her younger son, Richard, Duke of York, sought sanctuary at Westminster Abbey along with her son from her first marriage, the Marquis of Dorset. Meanwhile, her brother, Sir Edward Woodville, set sail with a small fleet and anchored off the east coast of Kent. It is thought that before he left, he had divided the late king's treasure up with the Marquis of Dorset. Richard offered a pardon to the fleet, which most accepted; however, Edward escaped with two ships and sailed to

Brittany where he joined with Henry Tudor. Around 15 May, King Edward was moved to the Tower, but this was not as sinister as it sounds, as at this time it was another royal palace. At the same time, Henry Stafford was made chief justice and chamberlain of both north and south Wales for life, and constable and steward of all the castles and lordships of Wales. It looked as if Edward's coronation was going according to plan.

Then everything changed. Richard must have become aware of plots against him, for on 10 June he wrote to the city of York asking for as many men as they could gather to assist against the queen, who intended to murder him. It was possibly not the first time, as it has been suggested that the Woodvilles intended to ambush Richard when they were taking the future king to London. Three days later, Lord Hastings, one of Edward IV's closest advisors, was accused of plotting against Richard's life during a council meeting and, without a proper trial, was dragged outside and beheaded. John Morton, Bishop of Ely, and Thomas Lord Stanley were accused of being co-conspirators and thrown in prison. Meanwhile, the late King Edward's younger son, Richard of York, was removed from sanctuary and sent to join his brother in the Tower; they were never seen in public again.

Richard then publicly declared his own claim to the throne. It began on 22 June when, according to the *Great Chronicle*, Dr Ralph Shaa gave a sermon from St Paul's Cross entitled

### Religion

Religion controlled every aspect of a person's life in the medieval period. Everyone was terrified of Hell and the people would have been reminded of the horrors awaiting them in the weekly services they had to attend. Excommunication and the denial of entry to Heaven was therefore the ultimate punishment.

'Bastard slips shall not take root' alleging that Edward's children were illegitimate and that Richard was the only true heir to the throne. Richard must have been expecting trouble because he proclaimed that:

> ... no man, under pain of imprisonment, should take any lodging in the city or suburbs, except by appointment of the king's harbingers; every one was to be in his lodging by ten o'clock at night; and the carrying of glaives, bills, long and short swords and bucklers was prohibited.

On 24 June, Buckingham addressed a number of London's leading citizens on the suitability of Richard to be king. The following day Richard was presented with a petition by a gathering of Lords Temporal and Spiritual and commoners asking him to become king. Richard of Gloucester was crowned King Richard III on 6 July 1483 in Westminster Abbey. His wife, Anne, was crowned alongside him and it was the first double coronation since Henry II, 175 years earlier.

# THE ARMIES

> The English are all good archers and soldiers …
> This nation is cruel and bloodthirsty and they
> even fight among themselves in the same way,
> waging great battles.
>
> Gilles de Bouvier, c. 1450

The English had built a fearsome reputation as soldiers during the Hundred Years War, with victories such as Crécy, Poiters, Agincourt and Verneuil which were celebrated throughout the kingdom. Many of the men who fought in the Wars of the Roses would have had fathers, grandfathers and uncles who would have taken part in these great battles. However, by the time of the Battle of Bosworth, after many years of relative peace under Edward IV, the number of experienced soldiers and commanders was dwindling. Those that did have experience usually learned their trade from fighting the Swiss and French in the service of Burgundy.

## Richard III

Born on 2 October 1452 at Fotheringhay Castle in Northamptonshire, Richard was the youngest son of Richard Plantagenet, Duke of York, and Cecily Neville. Following the death of his father and elder brother at the Battle of Wakefield, Richard and his brother George were sent to Burgundy for their own safety. However, after the Battle of Towton they were both recalled to England. At Edward's coronation in June 1461, Richard was created Duke of Gloucester and his brother George, Duke of Clarence. Although only 9, Richard was given liberal grants of land and office, including appointment as Lord Admiral. In 1469, when Richard Neville, Earl of Warwick, and his brother George rebelled against Edward, Richard remained loyal and was rewarded with a lifetime appointment as constable of England. In August 1470 Warwick and Clarence fled the country. The tables were turned when the rebels returned in October and forced Edward to flee; Richard was one of a handful of supporters who accompanied Edward to exile in Burgundy. Returning to England with Edward in March 1471, Richard, now 18, commanded the vanguard of the Yorkist army at both the Battle of Barnet and the Battle of Tewkesbury. Marriage to Anne Neville, Warwick's younger daughter, brought Richard more wealth and land. By 1480, thanks to his Neville connections, his brother's support and his own abilities, Richard had a loyal and extensive following in the north, which he governed on Edward's behalf.

*3. Richard III. (Author's collection)*

## Henry Tudor

Henry Tudor, Earl of Richmond, was the son of Edmund Tudor, Earl of Richmond, a maternal half-brother of Henry VI and Margaret Beaufort, a cousin of Henry VI. He was born on 28 January 1457 at Pembroke Castle, three months after his father's death and just before his mother's fourteenth birthday. As well as having a distant claim to the throne through his mother, Henry was also descended from the French royal family, his paternal grandmother being Catherine of Valois, daughter of King Charles VI of France. Henry spent his early years in Wales under the protection of his paternal uncle, Jasper Tudor, Earl of Pembroke. In September 1461, as Yorkist forces secured Wales for Edward IV, Pembroke fled, and 4-year-old Henry was made the ward of William Herbert, Edward's chief lieutenant in Wales. He was kept at Raglan Castle, where he was raised and educated with Herbert's children. When Warwick restored Henry VI to the throne in the autumn of 1470, Pembroke, once again, took charge of his nephew. After the Battle of Tewkesbury, Henry and his uncle fled to France; however, storms blew them off course and they landed in Brittany, where they were welcomed by Duke Francis II. In 1476, an English embassy under Bishop Robert Stillington convinced Francis to surrender Richmond. Henry was taken to St Malo where a ship waited to take him back to England, but he feigned illness and escaped to sanctuary in a local church. Henry eventually returned safely to the Breton court, where he remained in honourable confinement until Edward IV's death in 1483.

*4. Henry VII. (Author's collection)*

## The Commanders

Fifteenth-century commanders were expected to personally lead their men into battle and to inspire them with deeds of valour and personal bravery. The military experience and reputation of a commander, whether a king or nobleman, could boost the morale of an army and give it the edge in hand-to-hand combat. Unlike today, a commander did not have a bird's-eye view of events as they unfolded, and instead only had the height advantage of a horse or, if they were lucky, higher ground. Consequently, they would have seen little more than the enemy's front line, or if they were in the thickest of the fighting, virtually nothing at all. Nobles learned to fight from an early age, so by the time they reached maturity, using a sword or pollaxe was second nature. Similarly, being given their first suit of armour whilst they were very young also meant that as an adult, providing it was made especially for them, they could manoeuvre and fight under its immense weight.

Richard's training in the art of war began at an early age under the tutelage of the Earl of Warwick. His first real experience of warfare came in 1469, aged 16, when he accompanied the king as he marched towards Newark to deal with a rebellion led by 'Robin of Redesdale', a supporter of Warwick, the Kingmaker. However, the rebel army was larger than expected and Richard and the king were forced to retreat to Nottingham. His first independent command came in December the same year, when he was sent by his brother to deal with an uprising in Wales. As part of the campaign, Richard was given full power and authority to 'reduce and subdue' the castles of Carmarthen and Cardigan in south Wales, and to deal with the local rebels. Whilst he was in Wales, another rebellion erupted in Lincolnshire, instigated by Sir Robert Welles, another supporter of Warwick and Clarence. Edward successfully defeated the rebels at Empingham in a battle now known as 'Lose-coat' Field, and a few days later Warwick and Clarence were proclaimed traitors. It has been suggested that Lord Stanley, Warwick's brother-in-law, was en route to join Warwick when some of his men bumped into Richard, who was on the way to join his brother. A 'matter of variance' between Richard and Lord Stanley followed, although we do not know the details, and it would be the first of several altercations Richard would have with the Stanleys. Richard commanded the vanguard, which was on the right flank and facing the 'battle' (division) of Sir Henry Holland, Duke of Exeter. Richard immediately encountered difficulties when, on a fog-shrouded battlefield, he could not properly align with the opposite 'battle'. Eventually he found Exeter and, marching uphill, collided with it at an angle, hitting the 'battle' in the flank. During the hand-to-hand fighting that followed Richard was wounded and Exeter's men were chased from the battlefield. It would also be his first encounter with John de Vere, Earl of Oxford. Less than a month later, Richard's timely intervention against Somerset's 'battle' may well have been the deciding factor at the Battle of Tewkesbury when the Yorkists triumphed over a Lancastrian army led by Margaret of Anjou.

Henry, on the other hand, was the complete opposite; his first experience of battle as a 12-year-old boy saw him witness the slaughter of the Welsh nobility at the Battle of Edgecote, where he had to be rescued by Sir Richard Corbet (who would later join him at Bosworth). He was on the receiving end again in 1471, when, whilst at Pembroke Castle with his uncle Jasper, the castle was besieged for over a week by Morgan Thomas. No doubt he had some form of military training befitting his status, but he still lacked practical experience. However, like all military commanders, Henry would have formed a council of war, bringing all his most experienced commanders such as Oxford, Anthony Woodville and Philbert de Chandée together. It was these men who would advise Henry on his best course of action, although it may not have been until Henry met with the Stanleys that the final plans were drawn up.

## The Stanleys

Thomas Stanley, Earl of Derby (*c.* 1435–1504), was the ultimate fence-sitter throughout the majority of the Wars of the Roses. He even pledged his support to both York and Lancaster at the same time during the early stages of the wars. Whilst he was Duke of Gloucester, Richard was given land deep inside Stanley territory, creating friction between the two. It boiled over in 1470 when Gloucester, having mustered his retainers at Preston, marched on the Stanley mansion at Lathom intent on burning it down. The two sides clashed at Ribble Bridge near Wigan and Stanley not only beat Richard, but also captured his banner. According to legend, the banner was displayed in Wigan church until the Reformation.

In 1472, Thomas married Margaret Beaufort, Henry's mother. Three years later, he was summoned to take part in Edward IV's French campaign, and also Richard's Scottish campaign after that. In 1483 Thomas was implicated in the Hastings plot and arrested, although he was released in time for Richard's coronation where he held the royal mace. *The Song of Lady Bessy* tells us that Thomas went over to Henry on 3 May 1484; however, considering his wife was Henry's mother, he was probably involved at a much earlier date.

Sir William Stanley (*c.* 1435–95), Thomas' brother, was a staunch Yorkist, fighting for them at the battles of Blore Heath, Towton and Hexham. In 1465 he was granted the Skipton lands and Clifford Castle. In 1471, it was William who captured Margaret of Anjou after the Battle of Tewkesbury and he was made a knight banneret soon after. In 1483 he was also made chief justice of North Wales.

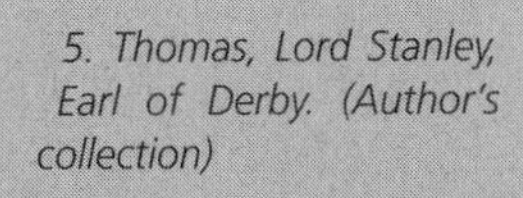

*5. Thomas, Lord Stanley, Earl of Derby. (Author's collection)*

## The Soldiers

There were four different types of troops on the battlefield at Bosworth: the spearman, the archer, the hobelars (light cavalry) and the man at arms (heavy cavalry), all armed with a variety of staff weapons. In addition, there would have been hand-gunners and artillery, possibly operated by mercenaries. The majority of the infantry would have been on foot, although there are accounts of mounted archers and of footmen riding to the battle before dismounting to fight.

The majority of the men at arms wore 'white harness', also called *cap-à-pie* (head to toe), but better known today as full plate armour. The men at arms, or heavy cavalry, were able to carve their way through the enemy at will, although it was customary for them to dismount and fight on foot as infantry. At the Battle of Edgecote, for example, Sir Richard Herbert 'acquited hymself, that with his Polleaxe in his hand (as his enemies did afterward reporte) he twise by fine force passed through the battaill of his adversaries, and without any mortall wounde returned'. However, as they were drawn from the upper classes of society their numbers were few.

It was the billmen and archers who made up the bulk of the army. By 1388 everyone was encouraged to practise archery and it became law that all artisans and labourers should practise archery at the butts (a target) every Sunday. Most would start as young children on small bows, increasing the strength of the bow as they grew, so that by the time they had matured they could use a powerful warbow. However, by the Wars of the Roses, archery practice was in decline, forcing Edward IV to issue a new statute commanding that 'every town should have a pair of butts for shooting, within the town or near it and every man at the same town between the ages of 60 and 16 shall muster at the said butts and shoot up and down three times every feast day'. They also practised fighting with other weapons, as Dominic Mancini

*6. Shooting arrows at the butt from a contemporary manuscript. (Author's collection)*

noted: 'it is a particular delight of this race that on holidays, their youths should fight up and down the streets clashing on their shields with blunted swords or stout staves in place of swords.' These men, with massive upper body strength from working in the fields since being children and highly developed muscles from years of archery practice, meant that there was a large pool of fighting-fit men that the nobles could call on. No wonder that Mancini records that 'their bodies are stronger than other peoples' for they seem to have hands and arms of iron'.

## Recruitment

The social structure of fifteenth-century England was still based on the feudal system of Anglo-Saxon times and was built upon by William the Conqueror, creating a strict pecking order where everyone knew his or her place. At the top was the king, then the dukes, earls, marquises, viscounts and barons, of which there were around sixty-eight. Below them came the gentry; the knights, esquires and some without any title, and numbered around 2,000–3,000. Next came the tenant farmers and servants of the nobles, whilst at the bottom were the farm labourers. Each was indebted to the level above for all they had. By the fifteenth century it was common to have a document drawn up that detailed an individual's military and civil obligations to his lord in return for pay, protection, land or other benefits. This document would be sealed with wax and then perforated or indented and torn in two, the lord retaining one half and the individual keeping the other. From this we get an 'indentured retainer' and a group of such men were known as a 'retinue'. Those closest to a noble would normally act as his bodyguards, both during normal duties and on the battlefield, and were referred to as his 'household'. Naturally, a lord would recruit his best, most experienced men as his retainers and it was not uncommon for an individual to be retained by more than one lord.

The other common method of raising an army was through a 'commission of array'. This was a written grant of authority from the king to appointed commissioners in towns or shires, who were normally members of the gentry, to gather all able-bodied men for military service. Notices would be pinned on church doors, but as few could read, they would be read out in town squares and in the churches. A commission of array consisted of companies, each typically comprising between fifty and a hundred men under the leadership of a captain. The companies were sub-divided into groups of twenty men led by a vintner (from the French '*vingt*', meaning twenty). The town was expected to supply and pay the men, and twice each year royal commissioners were given authority under their commissions of array to inspect and report on the military readiness of the county or town in their charge. The problem came when a man who was expected to be part of an array was also part of a retinue, especially if it was for the opposing side.

## Organisation

Sadly there are no detailed descriptions of how an English army was organised in the middle and late fifteenth century, except that it was normally split into three divisions or 'battles'. They were called the vanward or vanguard (sometimes just the van), the mainward or mainguard and the rearward or rearguard. The terms can be somewhat deceiving as the vanward could mean either the front or right-hand battle; it could also mean the battle with the best troops. Similarly, the mainward could be the centre battle and rearward the left-hand battle.

Another aspect we do not know is how the retinue and arrayed men were combined, if at all. Evidence suggests that arrayed men were divided into twenties, hundreds and thousands. This implies that they all fought together in one body, being the least experienced, although there is nothing to collaborate this. Being organised in this manner would have had its advantages, as it would have helped morale and allowed them to be more easily controlled by a commander. It is impossible to say how many arrayed men were at Bosworth or where they were positioned. Richard would have probably been unsure if they would stand and fight, so he may have placed his best troops at the front and the arrayed men at the rear under Northumberland.

The organisation of the retained men is equally elusive, although we do have some clues. Firstly, Burgundy and England were closely allied, particularly as its ruler Charles the Bold was married to Richard's sister. The Burgundian army was different from the English one in that it was a permanent standing army, opposed to one raised when needed. However, up to 2,000 English archers served in the Burgundian army at any time, and many English nobles and captains also served military apprenticeships there, taking part in the battles against the French and Swiss. This means that for the later stages of the Wars of the Roses, there would have been a pool of experienced men and commanders used to fighting within the Burgundian organisational system. We also hear from de Commines that their tactics were heavily influenced by the English, in that archers were placed together in one block and men at arms and infantry in another. Burgundian organisation, modelled

## BURGUNDY

Burgundy was the wealthiest and most powerful state in fifteenth-century Europe. During the Wars of the Roses, the principality was the chief rival of France. In 1468 its ruler, Charles the Bold, married Richard III's sister Margaret, where she had great influence until her death in 1503.

on the French system, was based on a unit known as the 'lance'. This was a man at arms supported by a swordsman, a spearman, three archers, a hand-gunner and a squire. They would then be grouped into *ordonnance* companies of a hundred lances. The main difference between the English and Burgundian (and French) armies was that both Burgundy and France had permanent, fully trained, standing armies, whereas most of the English were part time and only called for in a time of need.

We have a clue from two indentures, one dated 1272 for 'Ingram of Oldcotes', and another from 1388 for Sir Thomas Gerberge. These both say that the lord agrees to provide maintenance for the knight, his squire and, significantly, two yeomen. Another clue comes from details of Lord Hastings' retinue as he prepared to invade France with Edward IV in 1475. This document lists a number of his senior retainers and the forces they would be bringing. Beside each one is a number of lances and a number of archers. There is no mention of billmen on this list, although it is inconceivable that none were taken on such an important expedition. So where were they? Some historians have suggested that in this instance a lance means one man and that 'archers' refers to all the other infantry units. However, the list says Hastings was only taking forty lances and 300 archers, and Lord Grey of Codnor ten lances and 145 archers. This gives an average ratio of 7:1 archers to men at arms, which seems very high considering that at the height of the Hundred Years War a ratio of 3:1 was the norm.

*7. Detail of the Battle of Grandson from the Luzerner-Schilling showing staff weapons being used over-hand like axes. (Author's collection)*

We only have to look to the likes of the Duke of Buckingham, who boasted of a personal retinue of over 1,000, and William Stanley, who could muster 3,000, to see that these are small numbers for such high-ranking nobles. With all this in mind, a lance must have therefore been a group of men, the man at arms and perhaps a squire and two footmen, similar to the Burgundians, and common practice during the crusading era.

## Command

Each 'battle' would be commanded by one or two nobles. A letter from George Neville to Francis Coppini, a papal legate, written after the Battle of Towton describes their role:

> I prefer you should learn from others than myself how manfully our King, the Duke of Norfolk, and my brother and uncle bore themselves in this battle, first fighting like common soldiers, then commanding, encouraging and rallying their squadrons like the greatest captains.

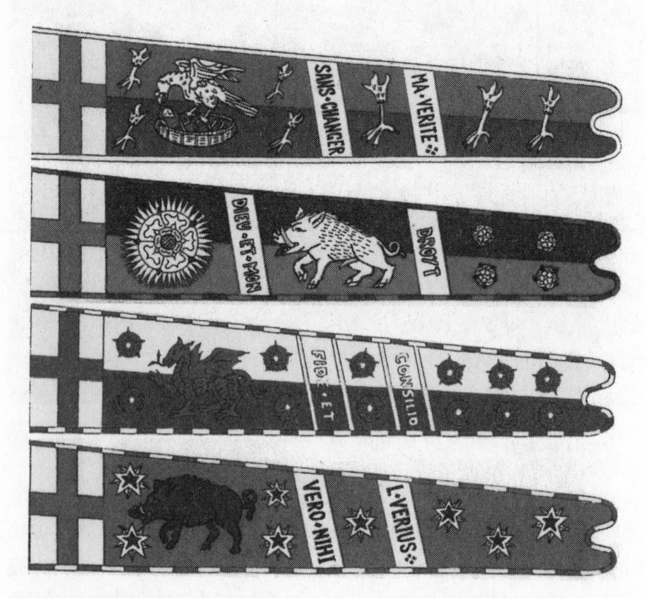


*From top: 8. Standard of John de Vere, Earl of Oxford, who commanded Henry's vanguard in the battle; 9. Henry Tudor's standard; 10. Richard III's standard; 11. Thomas, Lord Stanley's standard. (All Freezywater Publications)*

*12. Trumpets were often used to communicate commands. From a contemporary manuscript. (Author's collection)*

Controlling an army in the field was difficult at best, and although drums could beat time for a march or attack and trumpets could sound out commands, it was a noble's or a town's standard or banner that kept a force together. It not only identified where a particular unit was on the battlefield, but also served as rallying point, keeping men together in the confusion of a medieval battle. The most commonly depicted is the standard, which was a long tapering flag with either a rounded or swallow-tail end and showed the colours, badge, crest and motto of its owner. Its length was dependent on the status of the noble with the king having the largest at 8–9 yards (yd) long, whilst a knight's was just 4yd long. Some called 'Company Standards' were no more than 2yd long and 2 feet (ft) deep, but probably more common on the battlefield was the square standard or banner, which was stiffened and had a batten along the top to keep it unfurled. These would often show a heraldic symbol or badge on the livery colours, although it is recorded that one of Richard's banners at Bosworth was a 'Dun Cow' on yellow tarlatan (a form of tartan). It is probable that a noble would bring more than one standard or banner to a battle, and may have had variations to denote different units under his command. Towns would also have their own badges emblazoned on a banner. *The Rose of Rouen*, a poem about the Battle of Towton, lists some of these badges; for example, Northampton had the 'Wild Rat', Coventry the 'Black Ram', Leicester the 'Griffon' and Canterbury the 'Harrow'. Although in theory a banner should prevent two units on the same side from attacking each other, similarities could cause horrendous errors. At the Battle of Barnet, for example, Oxford's 'Star and Streamer' badge was mistaken for Edward IV's 'Sun in Splendour' by John Neville, Marquess Montague, whose archers fired a volley of arrows at the wrong side. Thinking that Montague had changed sides, Oxford's men retreated, leading to the collapse of the whole army.

Identifying the enemy and its movements was as critical then as it is today. Both sides would have used light cavalry as 'scourers', the medieval equivalent of scouts. At the start of the wars their usefulness was haphazard, but by the time of Bosworth they would have been experts at observation, liaison, shadowing enemy troops and securing advance positions. They could also be used to spread false rumours as to which way an army was heading. Although there is no earlier evidence of the light cavalry in the role, scourers acted as flank protection for the columns of men and wagons on Richard's march to Bosworth. Both sides also had intricate webs of spies, although because of the number of Henry's supporters that chose to remain secret, he was probably better informed of events in England than Richard was of events in France.

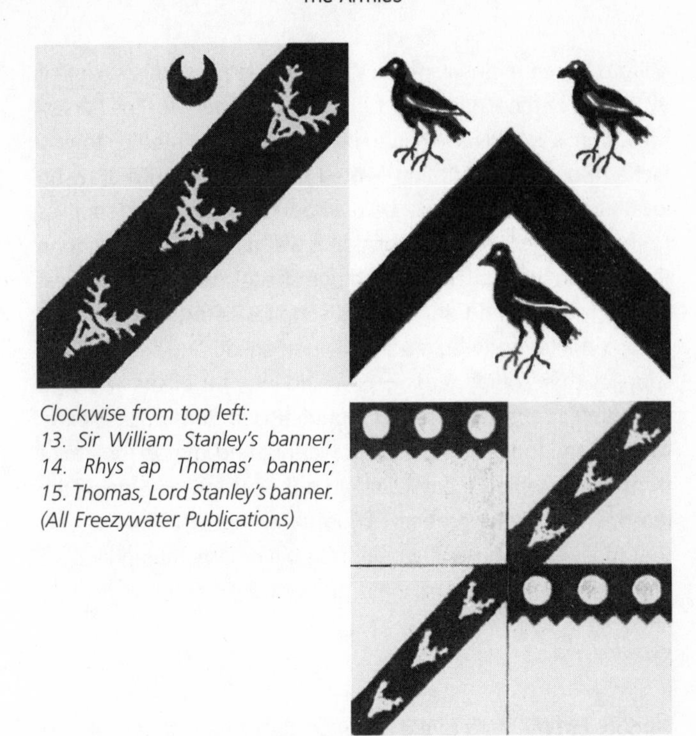

*Clockwise from top left:*
*13. Sir William Stanley's banner;*
*14. Rhys ap Thomas' banner;*
*15. Thomas, Lord Stanley's banner.*
*(All Freezywater Publications)*

## Logistics

> I have it on the best information, that when war is raging most furiously, they will seek for good eating, and all their other comforts, without thinking of what might befall them.

This was how a letter to the Venetian envoy Andrea Trevisan described the English in 1498. Although a man was expected to carry his own food with him on the march, it was likely that it would soon run out. Therefore, a good supply of food was essential in maintaining the morale and fighting capacity of the army, and even a small one such as Henry's could consume vast amounts. In the fifteen days it took his army to march from

Milford Haven to Bosworth they would have needed in excess of 97 tonnes of food, as well as 135 tonnes of fodder for the horses. Most of this would have had to be foraged or donated by towns. Richard, on the other hand, would have been able to draw on local supplies, and the night before Bosworth he received supplies from Coventry. Gregory writes that it was a matter of contention that the mounted infantry would ride ahead and take all the best billets, then eat and drink all the supplies before the footmen arrived. Victualers would normally ride ahead and secure what supplies they could; harbingers would look for billets and sites to make camps; and foragers would also be sent out for extra supplies and fodder. As a result, it was not uncommon for armies to march in separate battles along different routes. One of the reasons that Henry probably chose late August to invade was that most of the harvest would have been gathered and would provide ample food for his men.

## Kit

Throughout the Wars of the Roses, soldiers wore a tabard or coat in the colours of their lord or town, together with their lord's badge, or lord's livery, which was a mark of affinity. However, both Edward IV and Richard III tried to ban the wearing of livery coats. Throughout his reign, Richard repeatedly sent out instructions that only his colours should be worn or severe penalties would be handed out. So by the time of Bosworth, all Richard's army was probably wearing one colour, his colours being *azure* (blue) and *murrey* (purplish red). *The Song of Lady Bessy*, on the other hand, tells us that William Stanley's men wore red with a white hart badge, and Thomas Stanley wore tawny and green with a yellow eagle claw badge. We know that the French clothed Henry's men whilst he was still in France, so they probably wore Henry's colours of *vert* (green) and *argent* (white). We do not know whether the French troops wore the colours of their old unit or Henry's. As to those who joined him en route, they may have worn red or stayed with their own colours.

## The Man at Arms

In the fourteenth century, the most common body defence was a coat of metal plates, although, due to the limitations of manufacturing processes at the time, the plates were relatively small. Things changed in the mid-fourteenth century when larger furnaces and water-powered hammers were introduced. This

*16. A modern reconstruction of Milanese armour with a* barbute *helmet. (Author's collection)*

meant larger 'blooms' (a porous mass of iron and slag) could be produced, which in turn meant larger sheets of iron could be hammered out. From these technological developments, the first breastplates began to appear by the mid-1340s, and by the early 1400s a knight could be fully encased in armour. The main centres of armour production were northern Italy and Germany, although armour was also being made in France and Bruges. England had its own armourers as well, but little is known about them except that the Armourers Company of London received a Royal Charter in 1453. By 1425, having discovered how to harden armour, the Italians were making considerable improvements to their designs. Smooth round surfaces, limiting where a sword might bite, and two part breastplates, with the lower one overlapping the upper one to give double the protection, became features of their armour. They also added a smaller right elbow protector (*couter*), with the upper wing larger than the lower, and a larger reinforced *couter* on the left arm as well as asymmetrical shoulder guards (*pauldrons*).

In the 1460s, German armour manufacturers introduced the so-called 'Gothic armour' – a name given in the nineteenth century by historians because of its general resemblance to spiky 'Gothic' architecture. Gothic armour was characterised by its slender, elongated form, emphasised by ripple-like fluting with multiple laminations at all the joints to increase flexibility. Other features included symmetrical *couters* attached by arming points and symmetrical *pauldrons,* often with reinforcing plates (*gardbraces*).

The most common form of helmet during the wars was the *sallet* or *salade* (from the German *Schalle,* meaning shell), a close-fitting cap which extended to cover the sides of the face and the back of the neck. The *sallet* could be fitted with a separable and movable visor with a horizontal eye slot and it was constantly enriched with varied ornamentation. The bowl was forged from a single piece of steel so that the thickest part of the metal covered the forehead. Additional strength was afforded by a central ridge

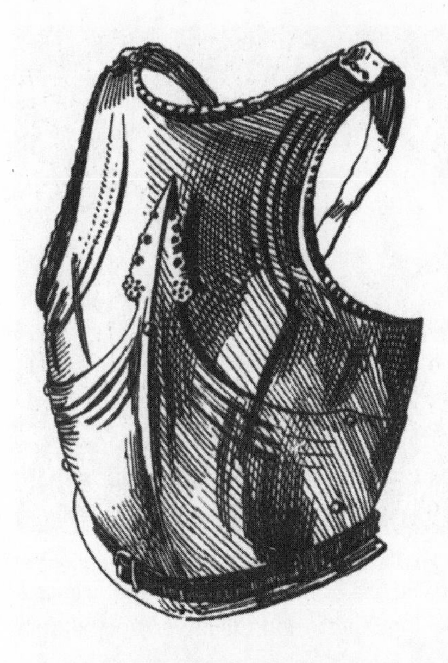

*17. Gothic-style breastplate with overlapping plackart for better protection of the stomach. (Author's collection)*

*18. One of the few surviving examples of English-style armour, taken from the effigy of William Martyn (d. 1503), at the church of Saint Mary in Puddletown, Dorset. (Armour Services Historical)*

*19. The Trevanion Sallet. Nicknamed the 'Bosworth Sallet' and thought to have been used at the battle by one of Henry's men. It has a one-piece raised visor and brow plate with laminated tail. (Armour Services Historical)*

which ran along the top, and an articulated tail-piece which protected the back of the neck. A plate known as the *bevor* was normally affixed to the breastplate and offered protection to the chin and neck.

Closely associated with Italian armour was a type of helmet known as an *armet*. These completely enclosed the head and, whilst being compact, was light enough to move with the wearer. The typical *armet* consisted of four pieces: the skull, the two hinged cheek pieces which locked at the front and the visor. A multi-part reinforcement for the bottom half of the face, known as a *wrapper*, was sometimes added, and its straps attached to a metal disc at the base of the skull piece called a *rondel*. Almost identical to the *armet* was the 'close helm'. This had a full visor and *bevor*; the visor pivoted up and down by means of bolts attached to the side of the skull piece. Another Italian design was the *barbute*. Resembling a classical Greek helmet, it had either a T-shaped, Y-shaped or arch-shaped opening, rather than a visor,

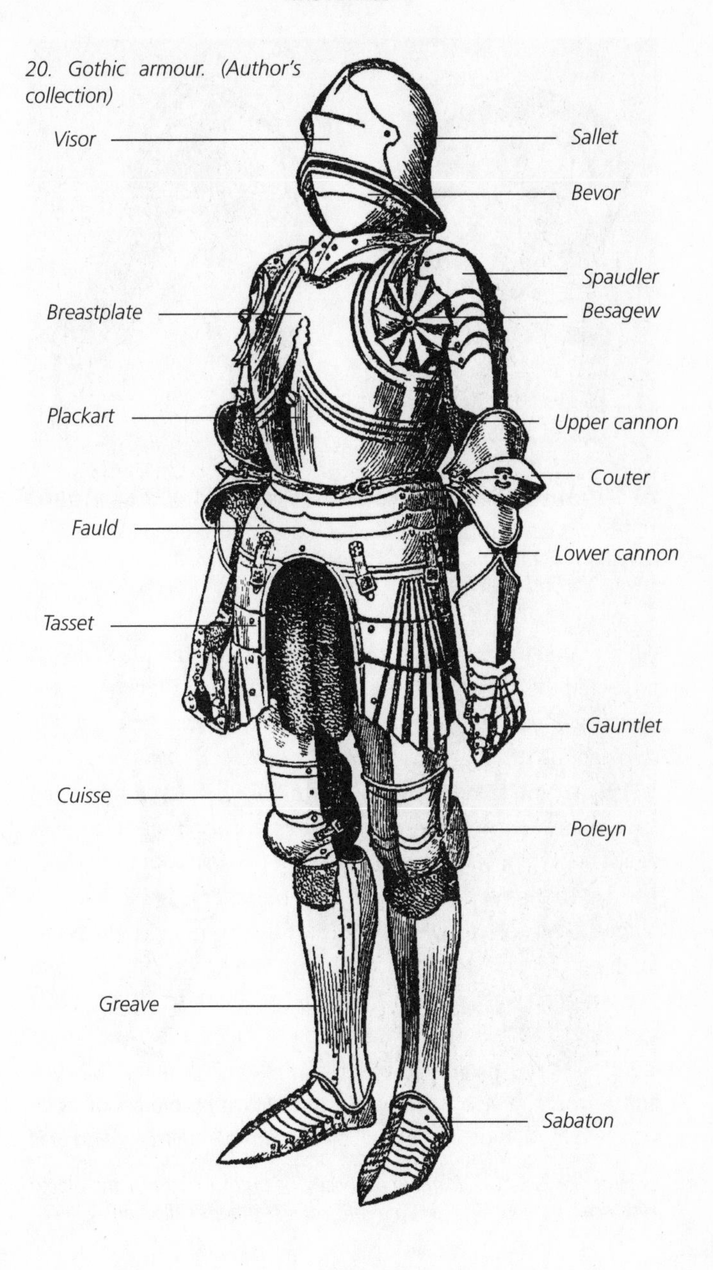


*20. Gothic armour. (Author's collection)*

*21. Two views of an Italian armet showing how it opened. (Author's collection)*

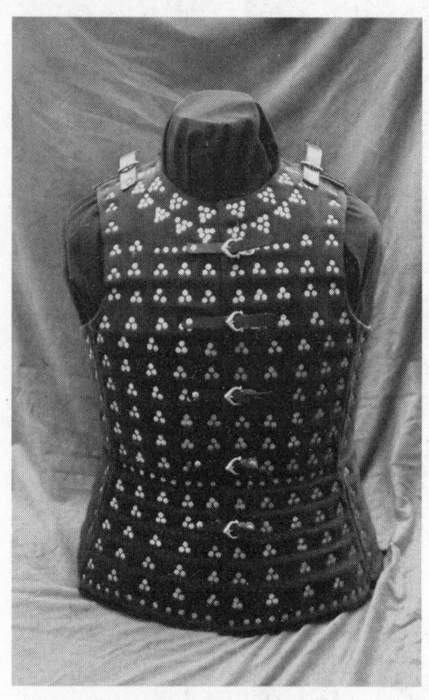

22. Brigandine. *Maison Tavel, from an original in Geneva. (Armour Services Historical)*

*23. Arm protection came in three parts, the upper and lower cannons and the couter to protect the elbow. (Author's collection)*

*24. Gothic-style gauntlets. (Author's collection)*

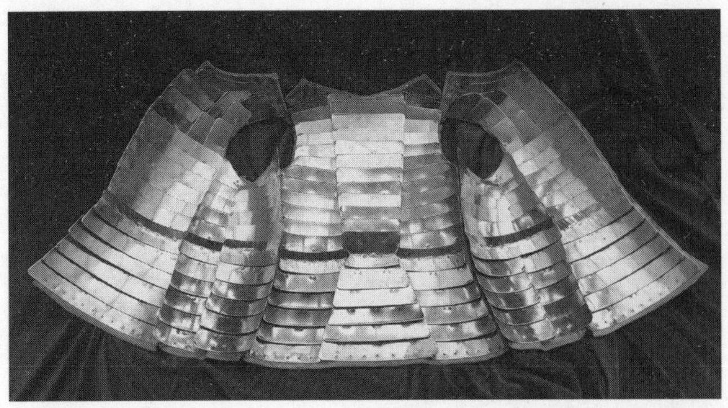

*25. Inside a medieval flak jacket called the* brigandine, *made from small plates riveted to fabric. (Armour Services Historical)*

and was made from a single sheet of steel, although by the time of Bosworth it may have gone out of fashion.

Whilst most armour would have been polished steel, there are examples of some having a blue finish from the heat treatment in the furnace. There is also evidence for a black finish, particularly in art, although it is not known if this is artistic licence or how the effect was achieved. There are also examples of *sallets* in Europe that are painted with one or two colours, either with or without script, while others have heraldic symbols. How far this practice was extended into England is not known.

## The Man at Arms on Campaign

According to the Hastings manuscript, written between 1450 and 1480, a noble or knight should take the following on campaign with him: a tent, a chair, a basin, five loaves of bread, a gallon of wine, a 'messe' of meat or fish, a board and a pair of trestles to sit his meat and drink on, a broad cloth, a knife to cut the meat, a cup to drink from, a glass with drink made, a dozen tresses of arming points, a hammer and pincers and a bichorn, a dozen arming nails (rivets), a spear, long sword, short sword and dagger, and a kerchief to hold the visor of his bascinet.

Another type of armour was the *brigandine*, which was the medieval equivalent of the flak jacket and was a cloth garment, generally canvas or leather, lined with small oblong steel plates riveted to the fabric. Many were faced with velvet, silk, fustian or satin. The rivets, attaching the plates to the fabric, usually in groups of three, were often made from gilt or latten and embossed with a design. These would have normally been worn with pieces of white harness to cover the arms and legs.

Underneath the armour a man at arms usually wore an 'arming doublet', which was a padded jacket with 'arming points' (laces) where the armour could be attached. Mail was also worn, but rather than complete coats, separate skirts, collars and gussets were made to protect the vulnerable areas not fully encased in armour. Some arming doublets probably had mail sewn under the arms for extra protection.

Even though a man at arms fought on foot, his war horse would have been his prize possession. The largest and heaviest, called a *destrier*, was around the same size as a heavy hunter today. Always stallions, they were bred for their stamina and thick powerful necks. There is also evidence that they were trained to lead with their right leg and to bite and kick. Of slightly inferior quality was the *courser,* often ridden into battle, and also a type called a *palfre*, which was used for the march. Therefore, it is probable that an individual knight or noble would bring at least three different horses on a campaign. To protect such a valuable possession, horses also wore armour called *barding*. A *chamfron* covering the head and a *crinet* for the neck were common, but they were also known to wear full plate armour, just like their riders.

The man at arms' main weapon was still the sword, but by this time they were becoming more tapered to find weak spots in armour. Without the need to carry a shield, they were also much longer and designed to be used in two hands. Due to the

*26. Mounted man at arms in composite Gothic armour with an equally well-protected horse. (Author's collection)*

development of plate armour, other weapons such as the pollaxe were becoming the weapon of choice. These had an axe head on one side and a hammer on the other. This could cause blunt trauma injuries as well as bend metal and lock up joints, and once an opponent was incapacitated, they could be finished off with the vicious square section spike on the top.

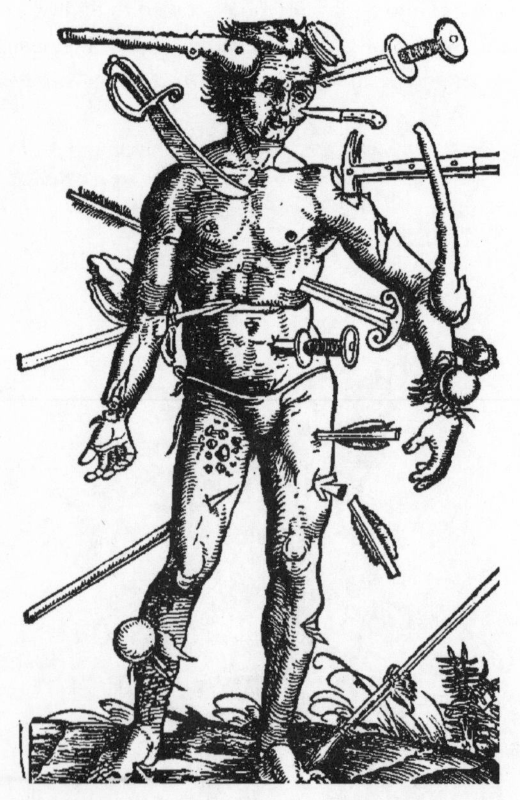

*27. The wounded man. A contemporary illustration showing the ways a man could be wounded in battle. (Author's collection)*

## The English Archer

The English archer was famed throughout Europe for his skill and effectiveness in battle. His D-shaped longbow was typically made from yew, imported from Italy and Spain, and was over 1.8m (6ft) long. Bows were measured by the strength it took to pull one, and the strongest could pull 72kg (160lb). The string was made from flax/linen or hemp and his arrows were around 762mm (30in) long and made from yew, apse (poplar) or birch. The 'fletchings' (feathers) were made from the primary feathers of a goose, and were 177–304mm (7–12in) long. There were a number of different arrowheads available: the 'bodkin' was long and pointed and used for piercing armour; the barbed dual-purpose arrowhead was effective against footmen; and the swallow-tailed 'broadhead' was used against horses.

He would have worn either a simple skull-cap or a close-fitting *sallet* with no visor, so he could pull the string back to his cheek and take aim. There are also numerous accounts of archers taking their boots off in battle, to get better purchase with their feet.

An archer could accurately shoot between twelve and fifteen arrows per minute at a range of 228m (250yd), shooting in high arcs down on to the opponents. Furthermore, once an opponent was within 90m (100yd) the archers could shoot direct into faces and weak points in armour with considerable accuracy.

*28. (Below) Reproduction medieval arrow heads. Not the piece of simple forged iron as once suggested, but sophisticated, heat-treated cutting tools that could penetrate all but the best armour. (Author's collection)*

*29. (Right) An English archer from the Beauchamp Pageant. (Author's collection)*

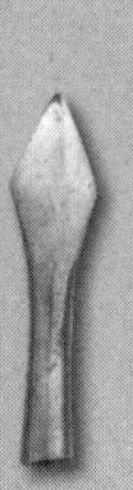

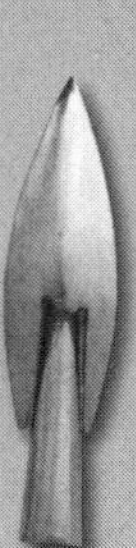

## Footmen

The ordinary medieval soldier would have worn his everyday clothes on campaign, which usually consisted of a shirt, doublet, woollen hose and boots. Most would have also worn a padded 'jack' for protection, made from layers of canvas or linen stuffed with tow, wool, straw or even scraps of mail. Mancini recounts that the softer a jack was, the greater protection it afforded. They were normally fastened down the front with laces and came either with or without sleeves, which were attached to the body by cords. The Duke of Norfolk's accounts describe his jacks as being made from eighteen folds of white 'fustian' (a coarse cloth of wool and linen) and four folds of linen. Another type made from small plates sewn into the jack and common in the next century may also have been in use as early as Bosworth. It was expected that every man should wear a helmet of some description, probably a *sallet*, while most would have also worn pieces of 'white harness', which would have been either a family heirloom, scavenged from a previous battlefield or given by a lord. Household troops would have been better protected than the common footman, with some wearing additional armour such as *brigandines*. This meant that no two men would have looked the same on the battlefield.

The most common staff weapons appear to have been the spear, bill and the halberd. The bill, based on the common agricultural billhook used for chopping branches from hedges and trees, had a pronounced forward curving blade, sometimes with a hook or spike on the back and often with a spike on top, mounted on a pole approximately 1.5–1.8m (5–6ft) long. It was a simple, practical weapon, unlike the longer, more ornate versions often seen today, which are based on guards' weapons from the time of Henry VIII. It would have been used much in the same way in battle as it would have been used in the fields and therefore required no training. This is supported by contemporary European

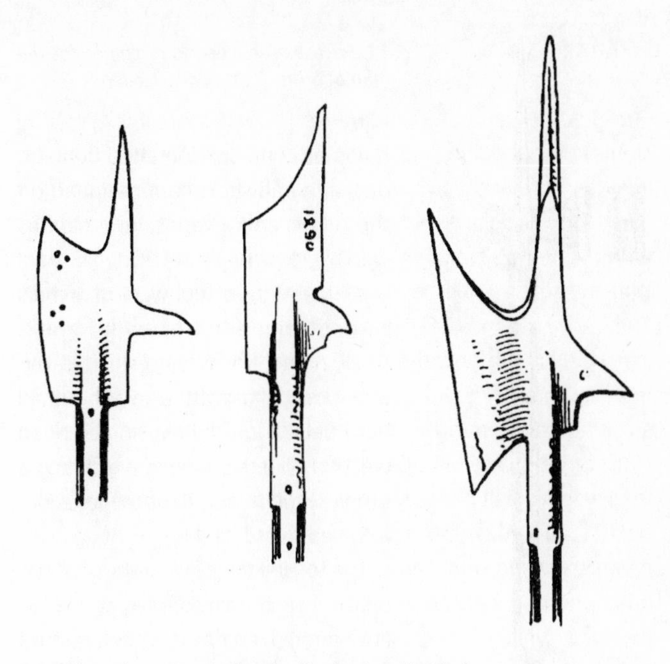

*30. Fifteenth-century halberds. (Author's collection)*

paintings which invariably show them being used over-hand. The halberd was a more sophisticated version of the bill, designed specifically for war, and had originally been developed by the Swiss in the thirteenth century. Two centuries later the halberd had evolved into an efficient weapon, with an axe head on one side, a beak on the other and a spike on top, mounted, like the bill, on a pole 1.5–1.8m (5–6ft) long. The halberd was probably as common as the bill, particularly with retinue and household troops. In the inventory of John de Vere, Earl of Oxford, after his death, there were 120 halberds and 140 bills, showing that he had almost equal numbers of each weapon. Other staff weapons that may have been seen on the battlefield include the *glaive*, which had a long convex blade; the *partisan*, a large triangular spearhead, sometimes with wings; the *bec-de-corbin* (Lucerne

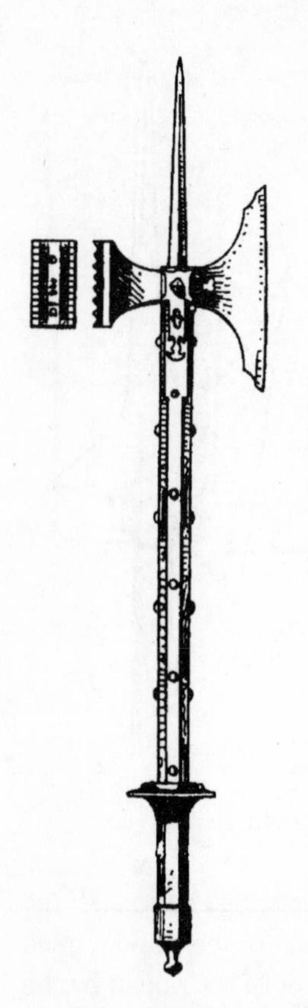

*31. Pollaxe. The weapon of choice for the man at arms. (Author's collection)*

hammer) with an elongated beak on one side and short hammer head on the other; and a variety of weapons with axe-type blades.

As well as his longbow, most archers carried some form of sword and a small, round, iron or steel shield called a 'buckler'. Most of the swords would have been short, heavy, single-edged weapons like the *hanger*, which had a simple knuckle guard, or the *falchion*, a curved sword.

The foreign troops in Henry's service, unlike their English counterparts, wore little armour except for a helmet and perhaps a breastplate, foregoing protection for mobility. Their main weapons were the longspear and halberd. The longspear (*Pique longue* in French), often incorrectly called the pike (a later term), was a 5–6m (15–18ft) pole tipped with a narrow, square head. It was developed out of a need to protect infantry from the heavy cavalry, much more common in Europe, and was ideally used in close, dense phalanxes, presenting a wall of spikes to oncoming cavalry. Some would have carried crossbows, although they were very slow to shoot (typically four bolts per minute) as they had to be drawn with the aid of a windlass; however, they were more powerful and had better penetration than a longbow.

*32. Crossbowmen and their protective shield called a pavise from a contemporary manuscript. (Author's collection)*

*33. Re-enactors portraying the French infantry at Bosworth; note the 16ft longspears, more commonly known today as pikes. (Author's collection)*

## Continental Style of Warfare

It was the Swiss who developed the use of the 'longspear' to fend off cavalry and break up infantry formations in their wars against Burgundy. Their tactics were so successful that they were soon adopted by the French, and then imitated by German mercenaries known as *Landsknechte*.

## Black Powder Weapons

We do not know what part black powder (gunpowder) weapons played at Bosworth, although we do know Richard brought an artillery train with him. *The Ballad of Bosworth Field* only gives two types of cannon: *bombards* and *serpentines*; however, there were many different sizes and calibre (bore) of artillery at this time, such as *crapedeaux*, *crapaudines*, *courtaulds*, *faucons* and *sakers*, as well as *serpentines*. The bombard was primarily a siege weapon of very large calibre; its purpose was to hurl huge stones at town and castle walls. Richard was not expecting to fight a siege, so it is much more likely that the bombard mentioned in the poem was one of the larger calibres of field gun.

It is not known with any degree of certainty when guns were first used in England, although they seem to be common by the 1320s and the word *canonys* (cannons) first appears in England around 1378. These early guns were cumbersome and difficult to use, but in the mid-fifteenth century there seems to have been a revolution in their design and use. Firstly, with the invention of the wheeled carriage, the cannons were made much more portable; secondly, improvements made to black powder allowed for a greater calibre of cannonball and range of fire. Black powder was a mixture of saltpetre, sulphur and charcoal. The saltpetre was imported from India via Venice, but by the time of Bosworth was probably made at Frankfurt in Germany and possibly in England as well. Sulphur was also imported, coming from two sources in medieval Europe – Sicily and Iceland. The fine, powdered mixture was confusingly known as 'serpentine powder' and was unreliable due to high water absorption of the saltpetre. How much was mixed in England and how much was imported already mixed is not known, although there was a 'powder house' at the Tower of London in 1461. Medieval guns took great skill to load: if the powder was rammed in too tight, it would not explode; too loose, it would just belch and the ball would roll out of the barrel; if the mix was wrong, it would produce coloured smoke, fizzle and bang without firing, or even explode, killing or maiming the crew. Gunpowder would not travel well either, as its constituent parts would separate if shaken, forcing it to be mixed again before use. However, in the 1420s a new process called 'corning' was developed; the powder was first made into a paste (often with the urine of a wine drinker) and then dried into balls or loaves which were then ground to a powder. This not only made it more stable, but far more powerful. It also meant different types of powder (sorted by grain size and by the ratio of its constituents) could be produced for different types of weapons. Both types of powder were still in use at the time of Bosworth, but corned powder may have been

*34. Early bronze cannon mounted on a wheeled carriage from a contemporary manuscript. (Author's collection)*

regarded as a 'black art', so it is not known how much Richard would have had.

There were also two designs of gun in common use. The cast-bronze gun, which was muzzle-loaded, had been in use since the beginning of the century, although the cost had made their use prohibitive until the middle of the century, after the price of bronze dropped dramatically. Trunnions could also be cast into the barrels of this type of gun, which meant they could be elevated much easier and give an increased range of fire. The other type, which had been in use much longer, was made from around ten wrought-iron bars arranged in a circle and held in place by iron hoops. This type was breach-loaded, with separate chambers into which the powder and ball were loaded. The chambers were sealed with a wooden plug, preventing the powder from separating, and then positioned at the back of the barrel. To ensure a good seal, a wooden wedge was hammered in behind the chamber. However, corned powder may have been too powerful for iron cannons, so serpentine powder was probably used.

Cast-lead balls were more suited to the iron cannon because the softer metal would deform to the shape of the barrel. However, when the cannon was fired, the wooden plug would also burst out, flattening the back of the ball, which necessitated an iron cube being cast into the ball to limit the deformation. Cast-iron cannonballs were also common, although to be effective they needed a smoother, rounded barrel, so were more likely used with cast-bronze guns. Only lead balls (mostly 60mm diameter) were found during the recent archaeological investigations at Bosworth, but this does not mean there were no cast-iron ones used, just that few probably survived in the soil (some may still be discovered). Richard would have undoubtedly had bronze guns in his artillery train, but just how many will probably never be known.

It must be remembered that medieval cannonballs did not explode, instead relying on their energy to smash through enemy

## MERCENARIES

Mercenaries were a common sight on the medieval battlefield. Usually coming from a foreign country, some were employed to make up the numbers, while others were used for their specialist skills as gunners or siege engineers. The biggest drawback when hiring these soldiers was that they could be tempted to join the opposing side for greater payment.

lines. Recent experiments with a 60mm lead ball have shown that with a flat trajectory (no elevation) they first impacted the ground at around 100m (109yd), before bouncing up to ten times to a distance of 800m (874yd). However, these tests were in ideal conditions, i.e. on flat, dry ground, while at Bosworth much of the ground was soggy from the marsh (which would have absorbed some, if not all, of their energy), and rose upwards from Richard's position, giving his guns a limited range.

By the time of Bosworth, hand-guns (*handgonnes*) had become commonplace. In Charles the Bold's army of May 1471 it is recorded that there was 1,200 crossbowmen and 1,250 hand-gunners. The English seem to have preferred to employ mercenaries as hand-gunners, with *The Great Chronicle of London* reporting that Edward IV had 500 'black and smoky sort of Flemish gunners' when he entered London in April 1471. Originally having a hook at the end, they were called a *harquebus*, or a *hakenbüchse* in Germany, *hackbut* by the English and *arquebus* by the French. These had a simple S-shaped trigger, called a *serpentine*, which fastened to the side of the gun stock. This pivoted in the middle and had a set of adjustable jaws, or 'dogs', on the upper end which held the smouldering end of a length of match that had been soaked in saltpetre. Pulling up on the bottom of the *serpentine* brought the tip of the match down into contact with powder in the 'flashpan', a small, saucer-shaped

*35. Fifteenth-century hand-gunner from a contemporary manuscript. (Author's collection)*

depression surrounding the touchhole on top of the barrel. After 1440, aiming from the cheek, or with a shortened stock propped against the shoulder, or over the shoulder, became popular, and gunmakers realised that a heavier, shorter stock was an effective means of absorbing recoil. Although there had been attempts to standardise sizes, they still varied greatly, with barrels typically between 500 and 1,000mm (20–40in) long and calibres between 12.5 and 16mm (0.50–0.65in). In the year before Bosworth, Richard had brought twenty-eight '*hacbushes*' (*hackbuts*) with frames, which implies they were of a larger bore and possibly mounted on tripods, as was common at that time.

Towards the end of the fifteenth century, the *serpentine* had started to be replaced by a mechanism, enclosed within the gunstock, that consisted of a trigger, an arm holding the match with its adjustable jaws at the end, a sear connecting trigger and arm, and a mechanical linkage opening the flashpan cover

*36. The type of cannon known as a hackbut on a wooden frame from a contemporary manuscript. (Author's collection)*

as the match descended. This was known as the matchlock and changed very little until the flintlock musket replaced it in the final years of the seventeenth century. In 1482, the Milanese fielded 1,250 hand-gunners, 233 crossbowmen and 352 *arquebusiers* (possibly referring to matchlocks). Another innovation at the end of the century was the pre-measured charge, which could be poured into the gun and greatly sped up loading. It is unclear exactly when it first came into use, although some may have been in use by Bosworth.

## Tactics

Warfare in the fifteenth century followed classical Roman thought, and no self-respecting commander would be without his copy of Vegetius' *De Re Militari* (*Concerning Military Matters*), written in the fifth century. An updated version, *Le Livre des*

*Faites d'Armes et de Chevalerie* (*The Book of Deeds of Arms and of Chivalry*) was written by Christine de Pizan in 1410. Another version written in ballad form was commissioned by Lord Beaumont and called *Knyghthode and Bataile*; it was presented to Henry VI shortly before the Battle of Northampton in 1460.

Fighting in three battles left few tactical options during the wars. With so many archers on both sides, the tactical supremacy of the archers during the Hundred Years War was largely negated; however, to leave them behind could have devastating consequences, as the Welsh discovered at the Battle of Edgecote. Here, separated from their archers, the Welsh infantry had to endure a relentless hail of arrows, with no way of replying; they were forced to charge the rebel army and were cut to pieces. Archers could be placed either with their 'battles' or, as at Bosworth, in a long line at the front of the army. After the initial archery duel, the archers would revert to their light infantry role and fight with sword and buckler. At the end of the day, all battles would have to be decided by 'hand-strokes' rather than the arrow.

This does not mean there was no room for ingenuity though, and surprise flank attacks were common. At Wakefield, after sallying out from Sandal Castle to confront a Lancastrian army, Richard of York was killed by just such an attack. Edward IV had expected an assault on his flank at Tewkesbury and hid 200 'spears' in a wood to protect it, before using these soldiers to charge into the rear and flank of the Lancastrian army. However, because of the effectiveness of the longbow, successful cavalry charges were few and far between in the wars in England, as the French discovered at Crécy and Agincourt, and Lord Audley found out to his cost at Blore Heath in 1459. The only time a cavalry charge could be effective would be if all the archers and infantry were engaged in hand-to-hand fighting, and the horses were given sufficient room to manoeuvre and gather speed.

Warfare on mainland Europe had followed a different path, with mounted charges much more common. As a result, the Swiss had developed the use of the longspear and halberd to counter ferocious charges by Burgundian heavy cavalry. The Swiss usually formed up into a *Gewalthaufen* ('battle'), which was a rectangular or square block, often with a *keil* (wedge) at its head. Along its edges, four ranks deep, were men armed with the longspear, whilst at its centre was a mass of halberdiers and men with giant two-handed swords. Against cavalry, they would form a 'hedgehog' with all the longspears pointing outwards,

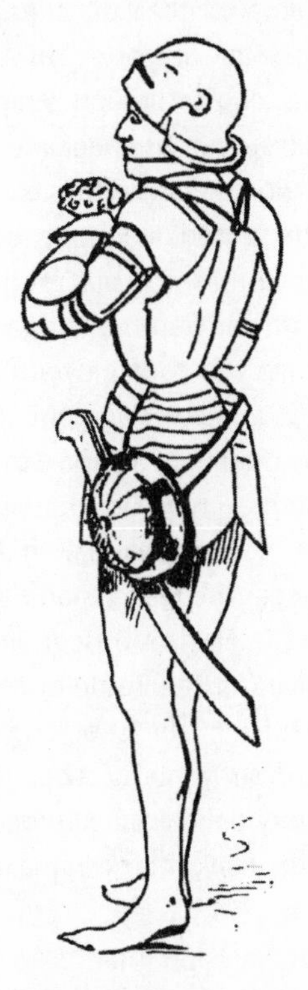

*37. A single-edged heavy sword known as a hanger and a small metal shield called a buckler were common sights on the battlefield. (Author's collection)*

and against infantry they would use the longspears to break up a formation, often from the rear or flank, before the halberdiers and swordsmen would rush out to attack the disorganised enemy. The *Gewalthaufen* would be preceded by a screen of crossbowmen and hand-gunners, who could then retreat behind the longspears for protection if necessary. These tactics were copied by the French in their wars with Burgundy and were used to great effect, especially at Bosworth.

Cannons and hand-guns were first used *en masse* in England at the Battle of Northampton in 1460. The Lancastrians had built a large protective camp for their guns, much in the same way as the French had done at Castillon seven years earlier. However, either through poor mixing or through damp, the guns proved to be ineffective. They were not used again in large numbers until the Battle of Barnet, where Warwick positioned them on his right flank when the battle started. In Europe, guns were sometimes placed in front of the infantry, but more often in prepared defensive positions on the flank. It had long been established that the most effective way to deploy artillery was in enfilade, i.e. across its longest axis or at an angle to the enemy's line, rather than head on, as armies were only several ranks deep and this would then reap maximum destruction. Christine de Pizan confirms this in her military manual, saying that firepower should be placed on the wings. The French had done this at the Battle of Castillon, cutting an English/Gascon army to pieces. Also, Charles the Bold's plan for the Battle of Morat in 1476 placed his artillery on the left flank, almost at a right angle to his battle line, in an attempt to destroy the Swiss before it reached his army. Throughout the century on mainland Europe, artillery continued to be positioned on the flanks of the battle, often behind ditches and banks.

# THE DAYS BEFORE BATTLE

Now is the winter of our discontent
Made glorious summer by this sun of York
William Shakespeare, *Richard III*, Act I, Scene I

1483

| | |
|---|---|
| **24 September** | Buckingham writes to Henry asking for support |
| **10 October** | The men of Kent launch their rebellion |
| **18 October** | The main rebellion starts |
| **19 October** | Richard hears of Buckingham's rebellion whilst at Lincoln and orders his army to meet at Leicester on 21 October |
| **23 October** | Richard's army marches south |
| | Buckingham's army is stopped at Gloucester |
| **29 October** | Buckingham is captured |
| **31 October** | Henry sails from Brittany to England |
| **2 November** | Buckingham is executed at Salisbury |
| **2 or 3 November** | Henry arrives on the coast of England, but, fearing a trap, returns to Brittany |
| **25 December** | Henry Tudor, Earl of Richmond, takes oath to marry Elizabeth of York, eldest daughter of Edward IV |

On 21 July 1483, Richard III left Windsor Castle for a royal tour of his realm, and after a few days a plot to rescue the two princes, who were still believed to be held in the Tower of London, was exposed. The plan was to set fire to parts of London as a distraction before storming the Tower. According to John Stow's *Annals of England*, the plot was led by John Cheney, esquire of the body and master of the bodyguard to Edward IV and Margaret Beaufort, while Robert Ruffe, William Davy, John Smith and Stephen Ireland were also involved. Over fifty conspirators were arrested and included men who had worked under Cheney in the royal household. It was also reported that they had been in contact with Henry Tudor as, even at this early stage of Richard's reign, plans may have been made to put Henry on the throne. In instructions given to Dr Thomas Hutton, who was sent to the Duke of Brittany to renew a commercial treaty which 'by diverse folks of simple disposition' was supposed to have expired in the death of Edward IV, is the following passage:

> Item, He shall seek and understand the mind and disposition of the duke, anenst Sir Edward Wydville and his retinue, practising by all means to him possible, to unsearch and know if there be intended any enterprise out of land, upon any part of this realm, certifying with all diligence all the views and depositions there from time to time.

Failure did not deter the conspirators and another plot was soon being hatched. This time it was centred on John Welles, maternal half-brother of Margaret Beaufort from the manor of Maxey in Northamptonshire, which he shared with his mother. However, the plot was soon uncovered and Welles fled the country to join Henry in France. Up until then, all the plots had been relatively small in scope, but unbeknown to Richard a full-scale rebellion involving the Woodvilles, Edward IV's displaced supporters and the Tudors, was being planned and would set large swathes of southern England against him.

In the meantime, Richard continued with his royal tour and by 8 August had reached Warwick, where he stayed for a week. The king must have been growing concerned as to who else would turn against him, for on 17 August he ordered Nicholas Spicer to assemble 2,000 Welsh billmen at Leicester, and for Buckingham to head a commission into treason. Little did he know Buckingham had already changed his allegiance.

## Rebellion

It is difficult to understand why Buckingham changed sides in support of Henry Tudor, as Richard had heaped titles and lands on him, making him one of the wealthiest men in the land. Vergil says that it was because Richard would not grant him lands formerly owned by the Duke of Hereford, but it is hard to believe greed was his only motive. After the 'Hastings' plot, John Morton, Bishop of Ely, was sent to Brecon Castle and into the custody of Buckingham. The silver-tongued Morton was a long-time ally of Margaret Beaufort, who played a significant part in earlier plots, and it may have been him who turned Buckingham. However, Hall suggests that Buckingham may have been involved in the plot even earlier, having met his second cousin, Margaret Beauchamp, on the road between Worcester and Bridgnorth. Perhaps whilst in his care, Morton played on Buckingham's vanities and told him all the conspirators wanted to see him on the throne? After all, he did have a claim to the Crown through Thomas Woodstock, the youngest son of Edward III. Perhaps it was a re-awakened desire for vengeance after the death of his father at the First Battle of St Albans in 1458 and his grandfather at Northampton in 1460? Or even his family ties to the Woodvilles, having married the dowager queen's sister, Catherine Woodville, over eighteen years earlier? No doubt the conspirators wanted him on board as a high-ranking figurehead and for his military strength. Buckingham claimed that he could field 1,000 men and John Rous reported that Buckingham had boasted that not since Warwick had so many men worn a single badge. Whatever his motives, Buckingham was firmly on board by 24 September when he wrote to Henry asking him to assemble an army and invade England.

By this time, Richard had reached Pontefract, where his son Prince Edward had joined him. From here they travelled to York, arriving on 29 September to a tumultuous welcome. Around the same time, he became aware of Robert Morton's (John's brother) and Bishop Woodville's involvement in a plot. He probably suspected Buckingham as well, as both the *Crowland Chronicle* and Vergil say Richard ordered a close watch on him.

Henry had been making plans for his return since early September, and Margaret Beaufort used Dr Christopher Urswick, her priest, as a messenger to inform her son of events in England. To help finance his return, Margaret also dispatched Hugh Conway (a servant of her husband) to Henry with a large sum of money raised in London. In addition, Duke Francis II of Brittany gave him ships, money and men, and according to Vergil 5,000 men were assembled at the port of Paimpol in readiness for the invasion.

The date for the revolt was set for 18 October 1483 (according to the later attainder). Men from Kent, Essex and Surrey would assemble at Maidstone, Gravesend and Guildford, and march on London in a feint, hoping to keep the royal forces busy, whilst others would gather at Newbury and Salisbury. The Bishop of Exeter and his brother, Sir Edward Courtenay, would lead a rebellion in Devon and Cornwall from their base in Exeter. Buckingham would lead an army from Brecon and meet with Courtenay and Henry Tudor, who would land on the south-west coast with a large army. However, it appears that through either impetuosity, poor co-ordination or communication, the men of Kent launched their rebellion on the 10th. Not only that, but they announced that Buckingham was their leader, drawing attention to his involvement. The Duke of Norfolk immediately sent 100 of his own men to block the Thames

## Act of Attainder

This was an act of Parliament whereby the faction in power could convict its political opponents of treason without bringing them to trial. It simply declared anyone named in the act to be guilty of treason and subject to the loss of all civil rights and the forfeiture to the Crown of all property. Because anyone so convicted was said to be 'corrupt of blood', all heirs and descendants of attainted persons were disinherited, thus allowing the confiscated property to be parcelled out among members and supporters of the winning faction.

crossing at Gravesend, preventing the men of Kent and Essex from joining forces, and gathered others to defend the capital.

Richard was in Lincoln when news of the rebellion reached him the following day. He immediately wrote to York saying that Buckingham had turned traitor and requested as many mounted troops as they could muster to meet at Leicester on 21 October. Richard also wrote to the Lord Chancellor requesting his seal, saying:

> And whereas we by God's grace intend to advance us towards our rebel and traitor the Duke of Buckingham, to resist and withstand his malicious purpose, as lately by our other letters we certified you our mind more at large; for which cause it behoveth us to have our great seal here, we being informed that for such infirmities and diseases as ye sustain, ye may not in your person to your ease conveniently come unto us with the same.

And in his own handwriting at the bottom:

> Here, loved be God, is all well, and truly determined, and for to resist the malice of him that had best cause to be true, the

> Duke of Buckingham, the most untrue creature living: whom with God's grace we shall not be long 'till that we will be in that parts, and subdue his malice. We assure you there was never falser traitor purveyed for; as this bearer Gloucester shall show you.

He remained at Lincoln for five or six days, making plans to crush the rebellion. Commissions of array were sent throughout England. Richard's leading nobles such as Lord Lovell also summoned their own retinues, all to meet at Leicester. We are told that Lord Stanley's son George, Lord Strange, left Lathom in Lancashire with 10,000 men, although his destination remains unknown. Some of these commissions would remain unanswered, however, as retainers such as William Stoner (a leading supporter of Lord Lovell) declared their support for the rebels. One of the biggest difficulties now was to judge who was friend and who was foe.

We do not know how many took part in the rebellion, but Stow says 5,000 men rebelled in Kent alone, and there were 500 recorded indictments in Exeter, suggesting that it was on a very large scale in the region. They came from all walks of life and from the 878 pardons issued afterwards by Richard, there was twelve nobles and over 200 clergy.

On 18 October, Buckingham unfurled his standard at Brecon Castle and marched on Weobly, the seat of Walter Devereux, Lord Ferrers, and gathered men as he went. From here he rapidly marched through the Forest of Dean, to Gloucester, where he intended to cross the River Severn and join with the Courtenays, who had raised their standard in the name of Henry Tudor and were marching from the west. However, ten days of continual rain had caused the Severn to burst its banks, smashing bridges and making fords impassable. Cattle, which were intended to provide food for the army, were drowned in their pastures, so the scarcity of supplies compounded his problems. Unable to communicate with or join Courtenay, Buckingham was forced to return to Weobly. Many of Buckingham's Welshmen viewed the failure to cross the Severn as a bad omen and, despite promises and threats, his army began to melt away. Meanwhile, Sir Thomas Vaughan of Tretower, who had probably been tasked by Richard to watch Buckingham, was advancing on his rear after plundering Brecon Castle. Buckingham fled, and we are told that he sought shelter at Lacon in Shropshire with Ralph Bannaster, 'whom he above all men loved, favoured, and trusted'.

As Richard continued his journey south, warships were stationed in the Channel to keep a careful watch for any ships approaching or leaving the country. He arrived at Grantham on 19 October, where he received the Great Seal in the Angel Inn, in the presence of Sir Thomas Stanley and the earls of Northumberland and Huntingdon. Richard then headed for Leicester, via Melton Mowbray, to meet his gathering army. By this time, the greater part of the south was in open rebellion. During his stay at Leicester he put forth a proclamation offering £1,000 or £100 a year for life, on the capture of the Duke of Buckingham; 1,000 marks (approximately £660) for the Marquis of Dorset (who had escaped from sanctuary and gathered an army in Yorkshire), or his uncle Lionel, Bishop of Salisbury, the son and brother of the widowed queen; and 500 marks on the arrest of other leading insurgents. The following day a vice-constable was nominated, and invested with extraordinary powers to judge and execute, without delay, any rebels that were captured or delivered into his hands. Richard and his army left Leicester on 23 October, arriving at Coventry on the 24th. On receiving news that Buckingham and Henry Tudor were to join in the south, he set off towards Salisbury.

Around 29 October, no doubt lured by the huge reward offered by Richard, Bannaster handed Buckingham over to the Thomas Mytton, sheriff of Shropshire. On 1 November, Sir James Tyrell and Giles Wellesbourne escorted him to Salisbury where, once in custody, according to *Grafton's Chronicle*, Buckingham named many of his co-conspirators and requested an audience with Richard, who had just arrived with his army. Richard refused, and on 2 November 1483 Henry Stafford, Duke of Buckingham, was summarily executed in the Market Place, Salisbury, possibly in the courtyard of the Blue Boar Inn.

Henry did not leave Brittany until around 31 October, no doubt delayed by the same storms that were hampering Buckingham. We are told that he had at least seven ships with 515 men on board each one. However, the storms scattered his fleet and only two ships reached England, which were anchored off Poole at the beginning of November. Unsure of what success Buckingham might have enjoyed, Henry sent a boat to reconnoitre the coast; a large group of men waited for him on the shore, saying they were Buckingham's followers and urged him to land. Henry erred on the side of caution, choosing to wait for more news. He then received word of Buckingham's execution; it had been a trap and the men on the shore were Richard's, so he raised anchor and sailed on to Plymouth before crossing the Channel again, landing in Brittany in mid-November. Without Henry or Buckingham, the rebellion faded away, without a pitched battle and little bloodshed. Many of the rebels quietly slipped out of England to Brittany and to Henry; however, Richard's troubles were only just beginning.

On Christmas morning 1483 Henry was in Rennes Cathedral, where he swore an oath to marry Elizabeth, eldest daughter of Edward IV, in front of his supporters. The unification of the houses of York and Lancaster was not a new idea and it appears that John Morton had discussed it with Buckingham during his incarceration, although Henry's mother, Margaret Beaufort, might have proposed it much earlier. For Henry, it meant that there was no going back.

## The Storm Clouds Gather

|  |  |  |
| --- | --- | --- |
| 1484 | **22 January** | Richard holds his one and only Parliament |
| | **April** | Richard's son, Prince Edward, dies at Middleham Castle |
| | **May** | Threat of a raid on Sandwich or Dover by Sir Anthony Woodville; Richard sends Lord Cobham to counter the threat |
| | | Border skirmishes with the Scots |
| | **June** | Henry escapes from Brittany to France |
| | **July** | Collingbourne's rebellion; Collingbourne is captured and executed |
| | **20 September** | Richard agrees a three-year peace treaty with Scotland |
| | **October** | Brandon's rebellion; the plot is discovered and the ringleaders flee to France |
| | **November** | John de Vere, Earl of Oxford, escapes custody at Hammes Castle and joins Henry |
| | **December** | Serious threat of invasion; Richard sends troops to Harwich |
| 1485 | **16 March** | Richard's wife Anne dies |
| | **Early May** | Henry is given the support he needs to launch another invasion |
| | **16 June** | Richard moves the court to Nottingham and prepares for invasion |

Richard was at Canterbury on 10 January and at Sandwich six days later. He then returned to London for his one and only Parliament. The Parliament met at Westminster on 22 January and King Richard opened it in person, with the Bishop of Lincoln, as Lord Chancellor, making the customary speeches. On the following day, the commons elected Sir William Catesby, who was a member from Northamptonshire and had been Richard's Chancellor of the Exchequer since 30 June 1483, as their speaker.

Eighteen 'private' statutes and fifteen 'public' statutes were passed over the following month. The first of the private statutes was the *Titulus Regius* (Title of the King), which reiterated why Richard and his heirs should be on the throne. Then, in the wake of Buckingham's rebellion came a series of attainders against those who took part, including Henry and his uncle, Jasper Tudor. The first attainder was against a total of ninety-two men across the south of England; the second act was just for the clergy, such as Morton; and the third was reserved for Margaret Beaufort. The remainder of the acts were related to the economy, including a series of statutes that sought to address the problem being faced by English merchants against what was seen as unfair foreign economic competition. Parliament was dissolved on 20 February and Richard headed north to Nottingham.

Richard had already begun to prepare for another invasion, for in December 1483 he recruited William Clowke of Gelderland as gunmaker and on 18 January made an agreement with John Bramburgh to make gunpowder. By this time, the use of cannons was becoming increasingly important on the battlefield, and twenty-five years earlier Margaret of Anjou had increased the royal arsenal to over 100 guns. Many of these must have been either lost or were outdated, as on 27 February Richard ordered seven *serpentines* on carts and twenty-eight *hacbushes* with frames. As the threat of invasion grew, Richard appointed Roger Bykeley on 5 March to commandeer all necessary workmen and weapons for the defence of the realm, and six days later appointed Patrick de la Mote, 'Chief Cannoneer or Master Founder', along with two gunners. Around the same time, he bought twenty new guns and two *serpentines*, as well as sending a large quantity of longbows and crossbows, with 400 sheafs of arrows, over 100 bow strings and 200 bills. The Cinque Ports, a series of coastal towns in Kent and Sussex, were ordered to send out ships to watch the movements of the Bretagne vessels, and a strong fleet under Sir Thomas Wentworth was stationed in the

Channel to guard the approaches to the English coast. Ships were purchased from the Spaniards to increase the naval force and extend its operations to the coasts of Scotland and France. John Lord Scrope of Bolton was nominated captain and governor of the fleet and commissioners were appointed 'to take mariners in the king's name, for the furnishing of the ships, and to do service upon the sea'. These ships were called the *Andrew*, *Michael*, *Bastion* and *Tyre*, and were destined for service in the north. It was one of the earliest instances of seamen being pressed into the king's service.

Tragedy struck during April when Prince Edward died at Middleham Castle, and all the accounts tell of how Richard was struck with grief. On 27 April Richard left Nottingham for York, where he is believed to have held a funeral for his son. Receiving more invasion threats, he first spent the summer at Middleham, then at Pontefract, Scarborough, York and Durham. In May, Richard received intelligence that Sir Edward Woodville was preparing to attack either Dover or Sandwich and sent Lord Cobham to the coast to counter the threat; several English ships and their captains were captured by the French off the north coast. There was also trouble on the Scottish border and Richard was forced to dispatch an expeditionary force to deal with it.

In Europe, Brittany was experiencing its own problems; there had been a number of French incursions on its borders and its ruler, Duke Francis, had been taken seriously ill. For a while at least, its treasurer, Phillip Londais, who was much friendlier towards the English, was running the country. They sent ambassadors to England, anxious to renew their truce. As a sweetener, Richard offered Duke Francis the revenue of the earldom of Richmond, which Henry Tudor had claimed for himself, and agreed to send John Grey, Lord Powys, and 1,000 archers to help defend Brittany's borders. In return, Richard asked that Henry be either placed under close arrest or extradited. Agreement was reached on 8 June and formally declared two days later. John Morton, who had escaped to Flanders in the aftermath of the rebellion, probably became aware of the plan through Margaret Beaufort, who would have heard it from her husband. He dispatched Christopher Urswick to warn Henry, who by this time had been placed under house arrest at Vannes, the capital of Brittany. On hearing the news, Jasper Tudor secretly crossed into Anjou, and two days later Henry and five of his followers left Vannes under the pretext of visiting a follower in a nearby village. Disguising himself as a groom, Henry and his followers fled into France, with troops sent by Londais hot on their heels. Duke Francis then allowed the rest of Henry's supporters to follow, also giving them 700 livres from his own purse.

Henry was welcomed at the French court and set up his own court-in-exile at Montargis in the Loire Valley after being given 3,000 livres to arm his men. By August he had over 300 supporters with more arriving every week, including Richard Fox, a noted cleric who was studying at the University of Paris. Not all the desertions were in Henry's favour, however. Thomas Grey, the Marquis of Dorset, had been with Henry since the rebellion and tried to escape back to England just before the invasion. Humphrey Cheney and Matthew Baker came after him, catching up at Lihons-sur-Santerre. He was 'persuaded' to return and had to remain in France during the invasion. Dorset never recovered his status after Henry was enthroned and was confined in the Tower in 1487, not being released until after the Battle of Stoke on 16 June. It is thought that Dorset may have been one of Richard's spies and was trying to warn of the impending invasion.

Relations with the French rapidly deteriorated and several naval battles followed. An assault on the last bastion of England in France, Calais, was also expected, but it never materialised. At this time, France was in political turmoil. Aged only 13, Charles VIII had succeeded to the throne of France the previous year; his health was poor and he was regarded by his contemporaries as of a pleasant disposition, but foolish and unsuited for the business of the state. In accordance with Louis XI's wishes, the regency of the kingdom was granted to his 22-year-old sister, Anne of Beaujeu, who was assisted by her 43-year-old husband, Pierre Beaujeu of Bourbon, and a council of twelve men. In May 1484 the king's closest cousin, Duke Louis of Orléans, and a number of other lords, supported by Duke Francis of Brittany, attempted to depose the regent. The insurrection that followed is now known as the 'Mad War' and it lasted until November 1485, when, by a mixture of diplomacy and shows of force, Anne succeeded in breaking the revolt without a major battle.

In a long proclamation dated 22 June 1484, Richard launched a blistering attack on Henry; it started:

> Forasmuch as the king our sovereign lord hath certain knowledge that Piers Bishop of Exeter, Jasper Tydder [Tudor], son of Owen Tydder, calling himself Earl of Pembroke, John late Earl of Oxon, and Sir Edward Wodeville [Woodville], with other divers his rebels and traitors disabled and attainted by the authority of the high court of parliament, of whom many be known for open murders, advoutres [adulterers], and extortioners contrary to the pleasure of God, and against all truth, honor, and nature, have forsaken their natural country, taking them first to be under th' obeisance of the Duke of Bretagne, and to him promised certain things which by him and his counsel were thought things greatly unnatural and abominable for them to grant, observe, keep, and perform, and therefore the same utterly refused. The said traitors, seeing the said duke and his council would not aid nor succour them nor follow their ways, privily departed out of his country into France, and there taking them to be under the obeissance of the king's ancient enemy Charles calling himself King of France ... the said rebels and traitors have chosen to be their captain one Henry Tydder, son of Edmund Tydder, son of Owen Tydder, which of his ambitiousness and insatiable covetous

> encroacheth and usurpeth upon him the name and title of royal estate of this realm of England, where unto he hath no manner, interest, right, or colour, as every man well knoweth, for he is descended of bastard blood.

And it concluded:

> And over this our said sovereign lord willeth and commandeth all his said subjects to be ready in their most defensible array to do his highness service of war, when they by open proclamation, or otherwise shall be commanded so to do, for resistence of the king's said rebels, traitors, and enemies. Witness myself at Westminster, the 22nd day of June, in the second year of our reign.

Richard's problems were continuing at home. William Collingbourne, a sergeant of the pantry under Edward IV and a tenant of Margaret Beaufort, met with John Turberville, a relation of John Morton, around 3 July in Partsoken Ward in London. Together they arranged to send Thomas Yate to Henry Tudor, requesting that he invade on the anniversary of the last rebellion. Collingbourne then posted a verse on the door of St Paul's; it read:

> The Ratte, the Cat, and Lovell our dogge,
> Rule all England under the Hogge.

The satirical verse poked fun at Richard and his chief advisors, Richard Ratcliffe, William Catesby and Lord Lovell. Although the exact date is not known, Collingbourne was caught and arraigned on 18 July, and was hung, drawn and quartered soon after, a method reserved specifically for traitors. Turberville, on the other hand, was only put in prison and appears to have escaped to Brittany.

At the end of August, messengers arrived in London from the French monarch, requesting letters of protection for ambassadors appointed to treat for peace; Richard issued them on 1 September. Meanwhile, sporadic uprisings were continuing in England, and around the end of October Sir William Brandon started an armed revolt that began in Colchester and spread into Hertfordshire. It included both his sons, Thomas and William, and Richard's own squire, John Risley. There is precious little information as to the events surrounding the revolt, except that it failed and the two younger Brandons, along with Risley, escaped to join Henry. Around the same time, Richard became aware of a plot to rescue John de Vere, Earl of Oxford, who had been held in Hammes Castle near Calais since 1475. Oxford had commanded the Lancastrian van at the Battle of Barnet in April 1471 and fled to France after Edward IV's restoration. It is probable that the two plots were linked as the indictments against the Brandons say that they were assisting both Henry and Oxford. William Bolton was sent to bring Oxford back to England on 28 October; however, he was too late as Oxford had persuaded the captain of Hammes, James Blount, to defect. Molinet suggests that Blount had been corresponding with Stanley about his defection for some time. They had both fled with John Fortescue, porter of Calais, to Henry in France, leaving the garrison, which remained loyal to Blount, in charge of the castle. Oxford was such a distinguished soldier that, according to Vergil, when Henry met the earl in Angers 'he was ravished with joy incredible'. Not long after the escape, Lord Dinham, governor of Calais, laid siege to Hammes. Oxford was soon to return with a relief force and whilst he attacked the besiegers from the rear, Thomas Brandon led thirty men along a secret path through the marsh and into the castle. It would be the following January before Richard would recover the castle, and only then after he had issued a pardon to those inside.

In September, whilst at Nottingham, Richard opened negotiation with the Scottish king and proposed a marriage between the king's son and his own niece, Lady Anne de la Pole, daughter of the Duke of Suffolk and sister of the Earl of Lincoln, whom he had nominated as his successor. On 20 September, the marriage contract was signed and a three-year peace treaty agreed. This meant that Richard's northern border was secure and he could concentrate his forces in the event of an invasion by Henry. By 10 November, Richard was back in the south touring Kent, before returning to London on 28 November.

At about the same time, Henry began to write to his supporters and potential supporters in England. According to Molinet, urged on by both Oxford and Stanley, he began to style himself as king, signing his letters 'HR' in the royal manner:

> Right trusty, worshipfull, and honourable good friends, and our allies, I greet you well. Being given to understand your good devoir and intent to advance me to the furtherance of my rightful claim due and lineal inheritance of the Crown, and for the just depriving of that homicide and unnaturall tyrant which now unjustly bears dominion over you, I give you to understand that no Christian heart can be more full of joy and gladness than the heart of me your poor exiled friend, who will, upon the instance of your sure advertise what powers ye will make ready and what captains and leaders you get to conduct, be prepared to pass over the sea with such forces as my friends here are preparing for me. And if I have such good speed and success as I wish, according to your desire, I shall ever be most forward to remember and wholly to requite this your great and most loving kindness in my just quarrel.

The king had only been in London a few days when information reached him that the French, despite their requests for a peace treaty, were trying to undermine him. In Windsor and other towns 'seditious manifestoes' appeared, instigated by 'false inventions, tidings, and rumours' emanating from sources in

France. Accordingly, on 6 December Richard addressed a letter to the mayor of Windsor, ordering him to check such attempts to foment discord and division between himself and his nobles:

> Forasmuch as we be credibly informed that our ancient enemies of France, by many and sundry ways, conspire and study the means to the subversion of this our realm, and of unity amongst our subjects, as in sending writings by seditious persons with counterfeit tokens, and contrive false inventions, tidings, and rumours, to the intent to provoke and stir discord and disunion betwixt us and our lords, which be as faithfully disposed as any subjects can suffice. We therefore will and command you strictly, that in eschewing the inconveniences aforesaid you put you in your uttermost devoir of any such rumours, or writings come amongst you, to search and inquire of the first showers or utterers thereof; and them that ye shall so find ye do commit unto sure ward, and after proceed to their sharp punishment, in example and fear of all other, not failing hereof in any wise, as ye intend to please us, and will answer to us at your perils.

This letter was also published as a royal proclamation in other towns, and one of its first consequences was the arrest of Sir Robert Clifford in Southampton. Clifford was given a quick trial, taken to Tower Hill and executed, but not before his supporters had attempted a rescue en route. Richard's mention of 'our ancient enemies of France' in his proclamation raises some interesting questions, as the French were publicly suing for peace with Richard at this time. With the political turmoil in France, it is unlikely that they were in a position to do anything, although clearly Richard thought that there was a credible threat of an invasion, dispatching Sir Gilbert Debenham and Sir Philip Bothe with a strong force to Harwich. But who was it that was going to invade, Henry or the French? And would anyone attempt a seaborne invasion in December? On 8 December, Richard issued a general commission of array, asking commissioners to perform a head count and to check that all men were well horsed and harnessed. He must have thought an invasion was imminent, as ten days later instructions were issued to the commissioner of array for the counties of Surrey, Middlesex and Hertford:

> ... to call before them all the knights, squires, and gentlemen within the said counties, and know from them what number of people, defensibly arrayed, every of them severally will bring at half a days' warning, if any sudden arrival fortune of the king's rebels and traitors.

Richard remained in London, but suffered another personal blow on 16 March when his wife Anne died, probably from tuberculosis. Rumours that Richard was going to marry his niece had been circulating since Christmas and this only served to fuel them. In reply, Richard was forced to make several very public denials.

At the beginning of May, Anne of Beaujeu finally offered Henry the support he needed to mount an invasion: a grant of 40,000 livres and a large loan. She also gave Henry a unit of between 1,000 and 4,000 French troops (depending on the source) under the command of Philbert de Chandée. These soldiers were all trained in the Swiss way of war with pike and halberd and probably came from the defunct camp at Pont de l'Arche. He was also given between 500 and 1,000 Scottish soldiers: the horse captained by Alexander Bruce of Earlshall; the foot by John of Haddington and Henderson of Haddington. If Sir George Buck's *History of the Life and Reign of Richard III*, published in 1646, is to be believed, it is also possible that Duke Francis sent an additional 2,000 auxiliaries, on top of his own followers, who by this time numbered in excess of 400 men; however, this cannot be substantiated. A fleet of around twenty ships commanded by Guillaume de Casenove (known as Coulon) was assembled at Harfleur on the mouth of the river Seine to take the army to England. Whilst his army and fleet were made ready, Henry waited at Rouen to meet his senior commanders. He would be leaving Sir John Bourchier and the Marquis of Dorset behind, possibly because the French needed hostages, but also because they could not be trusted.

With fresh threats of an invasion, Richard returned to Nottingham on 12 June, where he could respond to threats in any part of the country. On 22 June, letters were sent to Richard's sheriffs and commissioners of array instructing them to be ready to defend the realm against rebels and traitors, and another letter stated that all knights, squires and gentlemen should be ready at an hour's notice. Sir George Neville, son of Lord Abergavenny, put to sea to patrol the Channel whilst Lord Lovell and another fleet prepared for an invasion along the south coast. Richard could do no more but wait.

According to Grafton, Henry had a spy at the very top of Richard's administration: Morgan Kydwelly, attorney-general. Kydwelly warned Henry that Lord Lovell was lying in wait at Southampton and informed him that Reginald Bray awaited his landing at Milford Haven, with large supplies of money raised by Margaret Beaufort. He also advised him to land in Wales as soon as possible as this part of the kingdom was less rigidly watched.

On 1 August 1485, Henry Tudor, self-styled King of England sailed out of Harfleur to face Richard and take his crown.

## Invasion

| 1485 | | |
|---|---|---|
| | **1 August** | Henry sails from Harfleur to Wales; Richard is at Nottingham |
| | **7 August** | Henry and his army land at Dale near Milford Haven in Wales |
| | **11 August** | Richard hears of the landing and mobilises his army |

1485

| | |
|---|---|
| **14 August** | Henry reaches Machynlleth in Wales |
| **17 August** | Henry is at Shrewsbury |
| **19 August** | Henry meets Sir William Stanley at Stafford; Richard leaves Nottingham for Leicester where he will meet his army |
| **20 August** | Henry reaches Tamworth in the evening |
| **21 August** | Morning: Richard and his assembled army leave Leicester; Henry meets with the Stanley's at Atherstone. Evening: Richard's army arrives at Sutton Cheney and sets up camp |

Henry landed at Dale, near to Milford Haven, on 7 August a little before sunset; messengers were immediately sent ahead to inform the Stanleys and the Talbots of the landing. The next morning they marched to Haverfordwest, then, finding no opposition, continued for another 8km (5 miles). They soon received the welcome news that Pembroke was ready to support Jasper Tudor, their earl. The constable of Pembroke, Richard Williams, unable to stop their advance, raced the 322km (200 miles) to Nottingham to inform Richard of the landing. As the army reached Carmarthen, rumours reached them that Rhys ap Thomas and Sir Walter Herbert were barring their way. A unit of cavalry was sent to investigate, only to find Richard Griffith and a body of men waiting to join them, while Sir John Morgan and a few more troops joined soon after. We know little of the route Henry then took, except it was deeper into Wales and towards the lands of the Stanleys and not towards London or Nottingham as would be expected. This was probably to gather more men before a decisive encounter.

Richard received the news of the landing on 11 August. A small number of his nobles, such as George, Lord Strange, Thomas Stanley's son, were already at Nottingham. So too was the Spanish commander Juan de Salaçar, who under an agreement with the Holy Roman Emperor, Maximilian I, had arrived with a

## NEWS TRAVELS FAST!

Richard established a system of messengers where riders were positioned 32km (20 miles) apart. A message could be passed from one to the other, much like the Pony Express of the Old West. This way, any news could travel 100 miles per day.

unit of troops. Richard began to gather his army, immediately contacting his supporters and sending out commissions of array. He sent for Sir Robert Brackenbury, lieutenant of the Tower, who according to Vergil was told to bring Thomas Bourchier, Walter Hungerford and others Richard did not trust. He also summoned Sir Thomas Stanley, but he refused and claimed he had sweating sickness, although in reality he had either probably already left to join Henry or was trying to stay out of the forthcoming battle. Lord Strange tried to leave Nottingham but was caught. The *Crowland Chronicle* tells us that Strange then revealed to Richard that he, William Stanley and Sir John Savage had joined Henry. Lord Strange, probably under duress, then wrote to his father, describing his plight and expressing the need for him to come to the king's aid. Richard, in the meantime, declared Sir William Stanley and Sir John Savage traitors. By this time, York had agreed to send eighty men and Norfolk had ordered his supporters to gather at Bury St Edmunds on 16 August.

Henry continued his advance towards Richard and by 14 August had reached Machynlleth, having passed through Cardigan and Aberystwyth. On 16 August the ever-growing army, which now included Rhys Fawr Merududd and his men, camped at Welshpool. On 17 August they had reached Shrewsbury only to find the gates shut, but the timely arrival of Rowland Warburton, sent by Sir William Stanley, helped smooth the way forward; the rebels were now in England. Gilbert Talbot joined soon after with another 400–500 men; Sir Richard Corbet, Sir William Stanley's

*38. John Howard, Duke of Norfolk. (Author's collection)*

stepson, added another 800 men. On 19 August Henry reached Stafford and finally met Sir William Stanley, who was camped at Stone, 12km (8 miles) away, with between 3,000 and 5,000 men. From now on, Sir William Stanley was going to act as Henry's vanguard, staying ahead of the main army for the rest of the journey. Together they marched down Watling Street, the old Roman road, from which they could strike at Leicester or London.

On the same day, according to Vergil, Richard left Nottingham in square battle formation, reaching Leicester as the sun was setting. Here he waited for his army to gather. Men under Norfolk, Suffolk and Northumberland poured into the city, as did the men raised under commissions of array from nearby towns such as Coventry and Northampton; the latter commanded by Sir Roger Wake, Catesby's brother-in-law. Tradition has it that Richard stayed at the White Boar Inn (later called the Blue Boar) in Northgate Street, although it is possible that he stayed in the castle.

Henry's army arrived at Tamworth on the evening of 20 August, having passed through Litchfield. Here he was joined by Walter Hungerford and Thomas Bourchier, who had either escaped Brackenbury or were set free near Grafton Regis, home of the Woodvilles. According to Vergil, Henry was at the rear of the column with a guard of twenty men, which is somewhat unusual as the rear was the most vulnerable to attack and therefore not the safest place to be. At some point, he appears to have become detached from the main army and did not return until the following morning. Where he went is not known, although he told his followers afterwards that he had been conferring with 'secret friends'.

On Sunday 21 August Henry went to talk with Sir William and the newly arrived Lord Thomas Stanley, who were camped at Atherstone, and, according to Vergil, they greeted each other cheerfully and planned the forthcoming battle. No doubt they were aware that Richard's army was much larger and that they needed some kind of advantage if they were to win. So they decided to choose where the battle would be fought and to wait for Richard to come to them. They knew that Richard had to come down the old Roman road now called Fenn Lane and it just so happened that there was a marshy flat plain, with a ridge of high ground running parallel with the road. The marsh would limit the use of cavalry and reduce the effectiveness of Richard's artillery. If they positioned troops on the high ground, they would control the road and force Richard to fight at a disadvantage.

It appears from payments made 'by us and our company at our late victorious fields' after Henry had been crowned that the army was dispersed around the area. By late August the majority of the grain would have been harvested and would have provided a plentiful supply of food for the army. Atherstone, Witherley, Mancetter, Fenny Drayton, Atterton and the Abbot of Merevale Abbey all received compensation for loss of corn and grain, but it was Witherley and Fenny Drayton that were paid the most, suggesting that the bulk of the army was billeted there. It is not clear where Henry stayed, although some have suggested Merevale Abbey, a mile away from Atherstone; there is also a field just north of the town traditionally called 'Royal Meadow' so it may have been there.

There is tantalising evidence that an advance guard from Richard's army clashed with Henry's or Stanley's men whilst at Atherstone, as there are records of six men being killed on 20 August. These included Richard Boughton, sheriff of Warwickshire and Leicestershire. John Kebell, commissioner of array for Rearsby in Leicestershire, is also recorded as dying the following day. Also, on mid-eighteenth-century maps of the area, there is a landmark called 'Bloody Bank' just north of the town where the clash may have taken place.

Having been informed of Henry's location by his scourers, battle standards unfurled and ready to fight, Richard and his army marched over Bow Bridge, out of Leicester and along the Fosse Way on 21 August. Advancing towards Henry, Richard's army must have marched along Fenn Lane, stopping and setting up their camps on the top of the ridge of high ground the same day. From here they could not only control the road, but could also observe any movement on the plain. It appears that the majority of the army was camped either side of the road, outside the villages of Sutton Cheney and Stapleton. There was also a camp on top of Ambion Hill, although we do not know whether it was a small unit or a whole battle that camped there.

It certainly would have been an ideal place to observe Henry's movements. We are also told that once night fell, they could even see the fires of at least one of Henry's camps, probably at Atterton, which was only 5km (3 miles) away. A full-scale battle the next day was now inevitable.

# THE BATTLEFIELD: WHAT ACTUALLY HAPPENED?

The Winter's storm of Civil War I sing
Whose end is crowned with eternal Spring,
Where Roses joined, their colours mix into one,
And armies fight no more for England's Throne
*Bosworth Field*, Sir John Beaumont

Dawn came at 5 a.m. on 22 August, but before setting out Henry sent Sir Reginald Bray to meet with Thomas Stanley again, asking him to take command of his van; Stanley refused. According to Vergil he told Henry that 'the Earl should set his own forces in order while he would come with his array well appointed'. Vergil continues, saying that it was not what Henry wanted to hear and 'to that which the oportunytie of time and weight of cause requyryd, thowghe Henry wer no lyttle vexyd, and began to be soomwhat appallyd, yeat withowt lingering he of necessytie orderyd his men in this sort'. According to the *The Ballad of Bosworth Field*, Stanley then lent Henry four of his best knights: Sir Robert Tunstall, Sir John Savage, Sir Hugh Persall and Sir Humphrey Stanley, along with their retinues. However, we have a variation in accounts here, as Vergil says that Savage had joined the Tudor army the previous day. Beaumont says in

## Standard Bearers

The standard was the rallying point in medieval battles and identified the location of the king. The standard bearer therefore had to remain close to the king at all times and the position was considered a great honour bestowed upon one of the king's strongest and best fighters.

his poem, *Bosworth Field*, that the Stanley camp was also visited by Brackenbury and that he commanded the Stanleys to join Richard's army or else Lord Strange would be executed. Thomas Stanley replied that, after the death of Hastings, they did not trust Richard and that he had plenty more sons if Lord Strange was executed. Knowing that he had the support of the Stanleys, Henry then probably gathered his army at Witherley, as it was here that Henry knighted his standard bearer William Brandon and several other followers, no doubt to boost morale.

Richard, on the other hand, did not have a good start to the day. When he rose, he looked paler and more drawn than usual. Both Vergil and the *Crowland Chronicle* say he told his followers that he had a bad night, his dreams plagued by visions of evil spirits or demons, which Vergil ascribes to a guilty conscience. The *Crowland Chronicle* also adds that his chaplains were not ready to celebrate Mass nor was his breakfast ready, quite possibly because he was up earlier than expected. Richard may have had his faults, but he was unquestionably pious and would not have missed Mass. Tradition has it that he actually took his last Mass at nearby Sutton Cheney church, which even today still drips with Ricardian symbolism. If Edward Hall's chronicle is to be believed, Norfolk was given a warning of what would happen that day, for when he woke he found a note pinned to his tent that said:

Jack of Norfolke be not to bolde,
For Dykon thy maister is bought and solde.

Richard must have known that Henry was gathering his army. As Richard gathered his men, it was reported in the *Crowland Chronicle* that he told his followers that:

> ... to whichever side the victory was granted, would be the utter destruction of the kingdom of England. He declared that it was his intention, if he proved the victor, to crush all the traitors on the opposing side; and at the same time he predicted that his adversary would do the same to the supporters of his party, if victory should fall to him.

Another tradition is that he also drank from a spring at the foot of Ambion Hill before he set out, now called 'King Richard's Well'.

The majority of the chroniclers agree that some, if not all, of Henry's army had the sun behind them during the battle. As they were coming from the west, it means that it must have been fought, at least in part, during the afternoon, although we do not know what happened during the rest of the morning. Henry's troops probably took a while to assemble but, having learned of Richard's location, then advanced along Fenn Lane towards him. Encumbered by artillery and all the equipment of war, progress would have been slow. We are told that Henry had local guides, and although both John Cheyne and Robert Harcourt were local, we also hear of John de Hardwick from Lindley and a commissioner of array for Leicestershire showing them the way. The Stanleys, on the other hand, probably started out earlier, were travelling lighter and therefore would have moved far quicker.

We now know that Richard's army moved away from Ambion Hill and to get to the site of the battle they either had

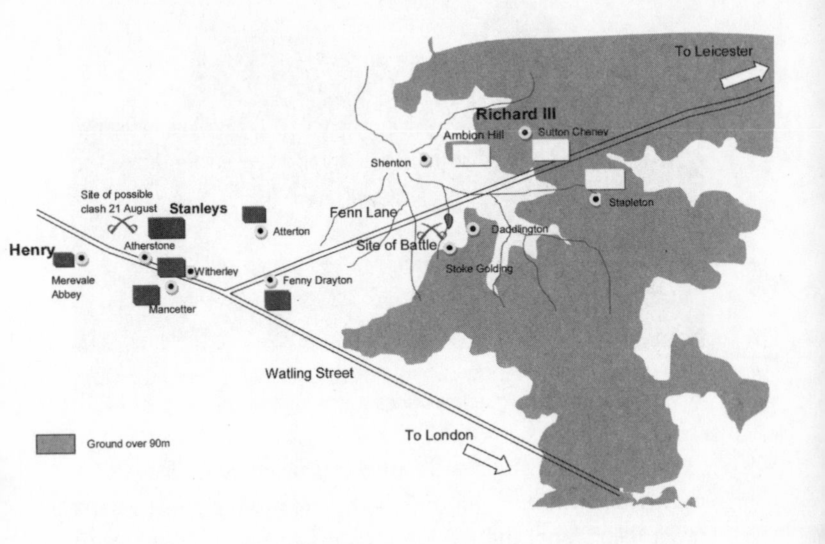


*Initial movements*

to move directly south towards Fenn Lane or more likely west to Shenton, and then follow the route south to Fenn Lane. A local tradition is that Henry was encamped at Whitemoors, which is just north of the battlefield and along this lane. This was probably due to finds associated with the battle during the seventeenth or eighteenth centuries but, given that it was believed that the battle was fought to the east on Ambion Hill, it would have been an easy assumption that it was Henry's camp. However, there could be a small grain of truth in this rumour, for if Richard had taken this route south, then it would be a likely spot to leave his baggage train before the battle. Why he would have taken this route or even come down off the high ground is unknown, because by going back along the ridge towards Sutton Cheney he would have retained the tactical advantage of the high ground. Perhaps he could already see troops massing there?

*39. Sutton Cheney church, where Richard traditionally took part in his last Mass. (Richard III Foundation inc.)*

It is possible that Richard's army was taken by surprise, for a manuscript written around 1554 by Lord Morley cites a report by Sir Ralph Bigot that said the royal chaplains were unable to perform Mass before the battle because of a lack of organisation. Bigot was present at the battle and as knight of the body to Richard and master of his ordinance, ranked highly in his household. He would also go on to serve in Henry's mother, the Countess of Richmond's household. Some form of religious service was expected before a battle and a processional crucifix was found near Sutton Cheney during the eighteenth century. So if this report is accurate, then only an unexpected and threatening situation could have caused the resulting confusion in Richard's ranks. Another version of events can be found in *The Ballad of Bosworth Field*, which describes Richard taking an oath in the name of Jesus and swearing to fight the Turks before his assembled army in true crusader style. Of course, any man undertaking a crusade would be offered remission for any and all previous sins, and by doing this Richard would have hoped to cleanse his past.

## The Battlefield

The area where the two sides met was centred on Fenn Lane, the Roman road to Leicester, and 3.6km (2.25 miles) north of the major Roman road of Watling Street. It was also at the junction of the boundaries of the medieval villages of Daddlington, Stoke Golding, Upton and Shenton, and 3km (1.86 miles) south-west of Ambion Hill. The ground was a flat plain, mainly comprising fenland crossed by streams, with an area of peat marsh, known as Fen Hole, south of the road. South of this marsh, the ground gently rises 20m (65ft) to a ridge that overlooks the road. On the top of the ridge is the village of Stoke Golding and approximately 600m (650yd) further north-east is the village of Daddlington. The ridge continues north-east towards Sutton Cheney, with a westerly facing spur now known as Ambion Hill creating a shallow valley enclosed on three sides, before falling 30m (98ft) back into the plain and the battlefield itself.

## Deployment

In working out the most likely way the sides deployed, we must first examine the sources. We hear from Polydore Vergil that:

> There was a marsh betwixt both hosts, which Henry of purpose left on the right hand, that it might serve his men instead of a fortress, by the doing thereof also he left the sun upon his back.

The find of the gilt boar on the edge of the marsh, found during the recent archaeological investigation, and Vergil's statement confirm the location of Henry's right flank. It also appears from Vergil's information that they were facing east and deployed north to south, at right angles to the Roman road, with the sun behind them. However, the recent archaeological survey has found a line of battlefield debris including a broken sword hilt almost parallel

*40. Looking towards the area on the battlefield where the boar was found. (Ian Post)*

to the road, which suggests the battle, and therefore Henry's line, was west to east. This makes little sense until it is combined with two other sources. Firstly, Jean Molinet says that the French were not part of the main army and that:

> The French also made their preparations marching against the English, being in the field a quarter league away … knowing by the king's shot the lie of the land and the order of his battle, resolved, in order to avoid the fire, to mass their troops against the flank rather than the front of the king's battle.

Then there is also a stanza in *The Ballad of Bosworth Field* that says:

> Then the blew bore [Oxford] the vanguard had;
> He was both warry and wise of witt;
> The right hand of them [the enemy] he took;
> The sunn and wind of them to gett.

*41. Looking west across Henry's position. (Ian Post)*

This is also supported in another ballad *The Rose of England*, which says Oxford made a flank attack, a common tactic at the time. So, if the ballad's 'vanguard' is the main body of the French, then it was these who had the sun behind them, and the east/west battle line then makes perfect sense.

Why did they deploy parallel to the road and not across it? For any part of Henry's army to have the sun behind them then part, if not all, of the battle had to have been fought in the afternoon. Richard may not have wanted to give Henry the advantage of the sun and arranged his army accordingly. However, it is much more likely that something, or someone, had forced Richard to deploy parallel to the road. This was most probably the Stanleys, who having arrived first had already assumed a blocking position on the rising ground overlooking the road, with whoever controlling the high ground taking a distinct advantage. *The Ballad of Bosworth Field* tells us that the Stanleys withdrew to a mountain where they looked across the plain and could not see the ground for men and horses. In medieval times, any high ground was called a mountain and the only high ground at Bosworth was

*42. Looking east across the battlefield towards Stoke Golding and Crown Hill. (Ian Post)*

where the land rises towards Stoke Golding, behind and to the left of Henry's army. This becomes significant when in another part of the ballad we hear that, as the two sides came together:

> King Richard looked on the mountaines hye,
> & sayd, 'I see the banner of the Lord Stanley'.
> He said, 'feitch hither the Lord Strange to me,
> for doubtlesse hee shall dye this day'.

Richard would only have wanted to execute Strange if he saw the Stanleys as an immediate threat, and what bigger threat could they have posed than being positioned behind Henry's army. Whilst the *Crowland Chronicle* does not say where the Stanleys were exactly, it does say that Richard ordered Strange's execution as the two sides approached each other. Another of

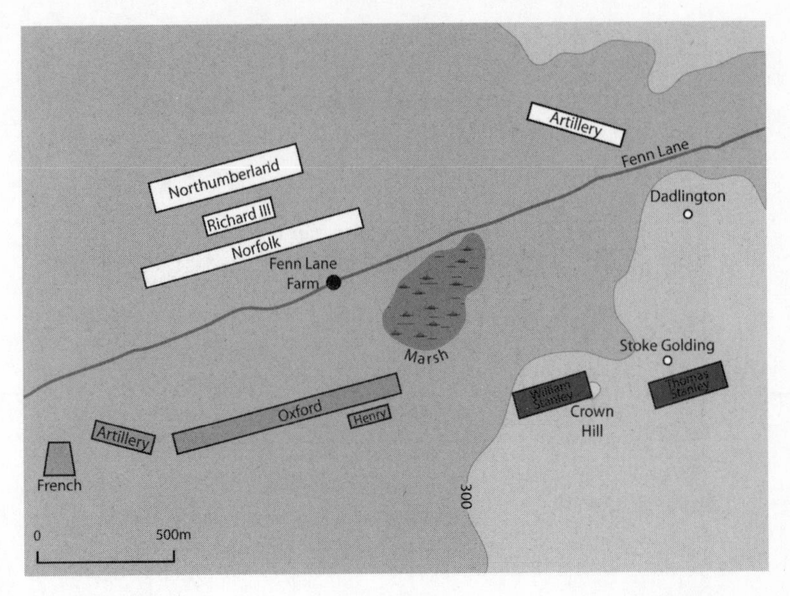


*First phase*

those local traditions says that marks in the windowsill of Stoke Golding church were made by men sharpening their weapons. Could these be from Stanley's men as they prepared for battle? So if we position William Stanley in the area around Crown Hill and Thomas further east near Stoke Golding, or behind his brother, together they could have blocked Richard's army from moving towards Watling Street or threatened his flank if moving west along Fenn Lane. If this is the case and they were in position before Richard arrived, then Richard would have had no alternative but to form up in front of the Stanleys, parallel to the road. It could be that it is this position to which Vergil refers when he says '… Thomas Stanley, who was now approchyd the place of fight, as in the mydde way betwixt the two battaylles, that he wold coom to with his forces, to sett the soldiers in array', because it would have been close to halfway between the two armies before they set out. With Henry's main army approaching

*43. Looking west across the battlefield, where Richard was initially deployed. (Ian Post)*

from the west and the Stanley's in front of him, Richard had been caught in a trap. Was this what the anonymous author of the note received by Norfolk was hinting at?

We must now turn our attention to the artillery. *The Ballad of Bosworth Field* hints at Richard's deployment of his guns:

> They had 7 score Serpentines without dout,
> that locked & Chained uppon a row,
> as many bombards that were stout;
> like blasts of thunder they did blow.

The chaining of the guns together in the centre of the line would have certainly hampered any movement by the infantry, but if placed on the flank, in enfilade, they could rake Henry's lines with cannon fire and cause maximum destruction to his ranks. They would also create an effective barrier, protecting the flank against attack. Additionally, they would also potentially be in danger of being dragged off by Oxford's men during the battle, so it would make sense to chain them together. There is also some physical

*44. One of the lead cannonballs in situ on the battlefield. (Author's collection)*

evidence to support this theory, as small groups of cannonballs were found close to the road, just where you would expect the guns to be positioned.

As Henry had fewer guns, it makes sense that he would have placed them as far as possible from the enemy gun line and on the left flank, as this would have helped to protect it without hampering troop movement. Having established the approximate positions of the battle lines, we can then estimate the position of the opposing forces' artillery by examining the pattern of cannonballs. The natural target for the guns would be the centre of the enemy's line, so with this in mind fields of fire emanating from Richard's and Henry's left flanks can be traced. In both cases, this would place them close to the roads and, as guns were heavy and difficult to move across country, this would be an obvious place to find them. This also is supported by Molinet's comment about the French attack on Richard's right flank, which would have been out of sight of the guns and their line of fire.

*45. A modern reconstruction of a fifteenth-century cannon. The separate breech (hanging inside the wheels) is fitted into the square block in the foreground. Wooden blocks hammered into place ensure a tight fit. (Author's collection)*

As to who was where, Molinet tells us that:

> King Richard prepared his 'battles', where there was a vanguard and a rearguard; he had around 60,000 combatants and a great number of cannons. The leader of the vanguard

> was Lord John Howard [Norfolk] ... Another lord, Brackenbury, captain of the Tower of London, was also in command of the van, which had 11,000 or 12,000 men altogether.

We therefore have Norfolk in command of the first line, probably with his son Thomas, Earl of Surrey, and Lord Brackenbury. Thomas had served a two-year military apprenticeship in Burgundy under Charles the Bold from 1466 to 1468 at the request of Edward IV, before fighting beside him at Barnet. It must have been an impressive sight as Vergil describes the vanguard as:

> ... stretching yt furth of a woonderfull lenght, so full replenyshyd both with foote men and horsemen that to the beholders afar of yt gave a terror for the multitude, and in the front wer placyd his archers, lyke a most strong trenche and bulwark.

Like the Battle of Towton twenty-four years earlier, it appears that all the archers were brought to the front, including Richard's yeoman archers. Only mentioned in passing was a number of hand-gunners, who were probably Burgundians under the command of Salaçar; they would have been deployed in the first line or on the flanks, and may have been in blocks or dispersed throughout the archers. When Vergil refers to horsemen it is not clear whether he means mounted or dismounted knights, although we know that knights usually fought on foot at this time and the action that follows does not sound like a cavalry action. If they were mounted, it was usual for them to be on the wings, and although Oxford's right wing was protected by the marsh, a short, sharp cavalry charge against the left would have devastated his line. An experienced commander like Richard would not have missed this opportunity unless something was stopping him: Henry's artillery. With both of Henry's flanks protected, negating any cavalry action, fighting on foot was the only option left for Richard's fully armoured knights.

To the rear of the vanguard was Richard and 'a choice force of soldiers', which would have included his bodyguard, household troops and personal retainers. Behind them was the Earl of Northumberland with what the *Crowland Chronicle* describes as a large company of reasonably good men. If Norfolk had all the archers and best infantry in the first line, and Richard was in the second line with his household, then Northumberland probably commanded the troops raised by commissions of array. These were, as previously described, raw recruits and would have had little or no experience of war. Vergil suggests that many would have changed sides or fled before the battle had begun had Richard's scurries not prevented them from doing so. Richard's array was therefore textbook Vegetius, with three battles one behind the other, used many times before in England and Europe. A number of historians have suggested that Richard's three battles were in a line, side by side, with Northumberland on the right. It has also been suggested that the reason that Northumberland did not get involved is because he was pinned in place by the Stanleys. Neither is likely, because firstly we are told that Richard has to move past both vanguards to get to Henry; we have already seen that the vanguard contained both archers and foot, and there is no mention of him passing Northumberland. Secondly, we are told that Northumberland should have charged the French, which would have been impossible if he was on the right flank.

Once Richard had formed up in battle array, Henry's army was free to form up in front of them. With such a long line facing him, Henry would have had no alternative but to match Richard's deployment, or face the risk of being enveloped as the longer line wrapped itself around the sides. We are told by Vergil that Henry:

> ... made a sclender vanward for the smaule number of his people; before the same he placyd archers, of whom he made captane John erle of Oxfoord; in the right wing of the vanward

> he placyd Gilbert Talbot to defend the same; in the left verily he sat John Savage.

As we have seen, the French were likely in a separate formation to the side or behind Henry's left flank. Henry was somewhere to the right of his line, probably behind the marsh, as Beaumont reports that he was in the shadow of the hill. With him was his personal retinue, which perhaps included his uncle Jasper, Sir John Byron, Sir Walter Hungerford and possibly a unit of French pikemen and cavalry. We are not told where Alexander Bruce and his Scots cavalry or the Scots infantry under John of Haddington were positioned; however, it is possible that the infantry were with the French considering the commonality of weapons and fighting methods.

*The Ballad of Bosworth Field* does confuse the issue when it says:

> theyr armor glittered as any gleed;
> in 4 strong battells they cold fforth bring;
> they seemed noble men att need
> as euer came to maintaine [a] King.

The most likely explanation for this is that the author is referring to Henry's army and the four 'battles' are Oxford's, the French and the two Stanleys'. This then supports the theory that the French were separate and that the Stanleys had already declared their allegiance to Henry. It was a common Swiss and French tactic to form up in four 'battles', in echelon (obliquely), and was successfully employed by the Swiss at the Battle of Morat nine years earlier. Richard may have had the larger army, but Henry already had two advantages: his right flank was protected by the marsh, and he was on the higher ground. Both limited the effects of Richard's superior artillery, for, as we have seen, a cannon's maximum range was attained through the ball bouncing over firm ground, and cannonballs do not bounce well in marsh or uphill.

We do not know how many men faced each other that day, as medieval chroniclers always appear to be wildly inaccurate when estimating how many men fought in a battle. Molinet puts Richard's army as having 60,000 men and *The Ballad of Bosworth Field* says 40,000. Only Vergil gives the size of Henry's army, which he puts at 5,000 men, and comments that Richard had at least twice as many.

The confused *Castilian Report* says that Richard's vanguard had both 7,000 and 10,000 men at different points, and Molinet says it was 11,000 or 12,000. The length of the line of battlefield debris found during the recent investigations is around 914m (1,000yd), so the two vanguards must have been at least this long. Assuming that there were no gaps in the vanguards and that men require a metre of space each when fighting side by side, then we can estimate that there were around 1,000 men in the front line of the two vanguards. Norfolk would also have had at least two or three ranks of archers and at least three ranks of infantry and knights, so there must have been a minimum total of 5,000 men in the vanguard. However, the vanguard could easily have been ten ranks deep given that the royal yeoman archers alone had raised 3,000 men in the past, meaning that 10,000 men is not outside the realms of possibility. Not one source gives the number of men in Richard's 'battle', but in all probability it was comparatively small as the majority of his archers were in the vanguard. Only Molinet gives a total of 10,000 men under Northumberland, although this is probably an exaggeration. We can therefore estimate that Richard's army had between 10,000 and 15,000 men in total.

We are told that Henry's vanguard was slender, but that it also matched Norfolk's in length. It is unlikely that the men were deployed less than three or four men deep, or 3,000–4,000 men, as a line only two men deep would be quickly overrun by the superior numbers of Richard's forces. With the French in their separate formation and consisting of approximately 1,000 men,

*46. The battle started with an archery duel. (Author's collection)*

Vergil's estimation of 5,000 men could be close to the truth. Sources vary widely as to the size of Stanley's force, with de Commines saying that Stanley brought Henry 26,000 men, whilst Vergil estimated William Stanley's forces at 3,000 men.

## The Battle

A number of historians have described the battle as a clash between the old style of warfare, espoused by Richard, and the new style of warfare learnt by Henry during his time on the Continent. It is also believed that Richard did not know how to respond to Henry's tactics, although given that many of Richard's men had been fighting on the Continent and that Salaçar was newly arrived from Europe, this was almost certainly not the case.

Henry must have advanced on Richard first, as the *Crowland Chronicle* says that 'the earl of Richmond with his men proceeded directly against King Richard'. No doubt Richard's artillery opened fire as soon as they were in range and Norfolk's archers would have followed suit. With the likely amount of firepower arrayed against them, Henry's men had no alternative but to advance or else be destroyed where they stood. Then, when Richard saw Henry's army passing the marsh:

> ... he commandyd his soldiers to geave charge uppon them. They making suddanely great showtes assaultyd the enemy first with arrowes, who wer nothing faynt unto the fyght but began also to shoote fearcely; but whan they cam to hand strokes the matter than was delt with blades.

Norfolk's and Henry's archers exchanged fire as they charged to meet each other, before grasping their bucklers and drawing their swords ready for the hand-to-hand fighting to come. Medieval warfare was bloody and brutal, and with a resounding crash the two sides met: swords slashing, bills and halberds chopping and stabbing, arrows flying through the air as archers continued to take potshots at the mass of men. The fully armoured knights and their retinues followed behind, carving their way through the lightly armoured men with sword or pollaxe, looking for equals. Small groups of lightly armoured men isolated and pinned down heavily armoured opponents looking for chinks in their armour so they could deliver the *coup de grâce*. The noise must have been deafening as metal clashed with metal, mingled with shouts and cries, and the roar of cannon and hand-gun; the whole scene shrouded in a fog of gunpowder smoke.

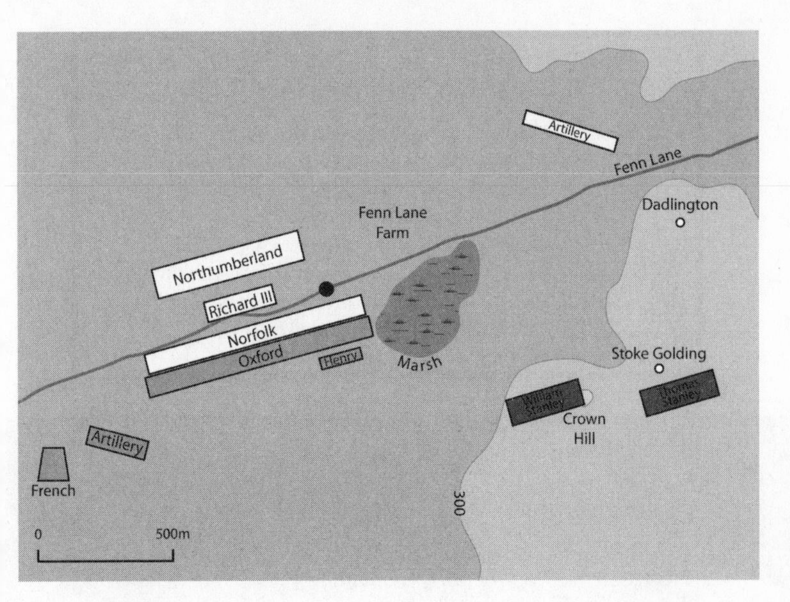


*Second phase*

The two sides then disengaged, although why they did this is not clear. Perhaps, as modern research suggests was necessary for all medieval battles, both sides paused for breath and regrouped under their lords' standards. It may have been because Oxford's division was being beaten and he was in fear of being enveloped, as Vergil tells us:

> ... fearing lest hys men in fyghting might be envyronyd of the multitude, commandyd in every rang that no soldiers should go above tenfoote from the standerds ... with the bandes of men closse one to an other, gave freshe charge uppon thenemy, and in array tryangle vehemently renewyd the conflict.

However, re-forming the soldiers into triangular or wedge formations sounds more like a pre-arranged plan, and after Oxford's division had re-formed they charged again. It was

## Death on the Battlefield

Although many would have died on the battlefield from horrifying wounds and loss of blood, many more would have died in the days that followed from blood poisoning and gangrene. One of the main causes of this was from arrows, which had been planted in the ground beside an archer. The archer would then go to the toilet where he stood, adding to the bacteria and germs in the ground.

*47. After the archery duel, Richard's army charged and vicious hand-to-hand fighting followed. (Author's collection)*

probably at this point that the French suddenly appeared on Norfolk's right flank, with the sun behind them. Bristling with 5m (16ft) longspears and screened by hand-gunners and crossbowmen, they crashed into Norfolk's line and began to break it apart. Further evidence of this can be found in a fragment of a letter written by a Frenchman soon after the battle. This long-lost letter, which was quoted in a paper written by Alfred Spont in 1897, claims that Richard had shouted: 'These French traitors are today the cause of our realm's ruin.' The only way that the French could have been stopped was either with the artillery, which was on the opposite flank, or the archers and hand-gunners, who were engaged in hand-to-hand fighting to their front. A third option would have been to charge them with Richard's cavalry; however, against the pikes the chances of success were slim. The French were, in effect, unstoppable and Richard had been outmanoeuvred.

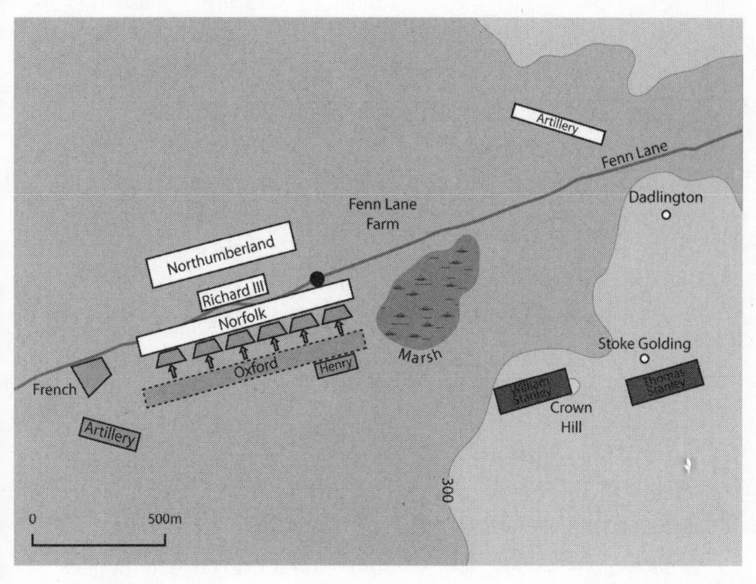


*Third phase*

*48. Richard had a contingent of hand-gunners, possibly from Burgundy, in his army. Wildly inaccurate, slow and cumbersome, but deadly at close range. (Author's collection)*

It was during this assault that Norfolk was probably killed, although *The Song of Lady Bessy* says he was killed by John Savage close to Daddlington Mill. Beaumont gives an entirely different perspective in his poem, saying that Norfolk recognised Oxford by his standard, a star with rays, and charged him. He continues to describe how the lances of the two crossed and shivered as they struck the armour of the other. Renewing the combat with their swords, Norfolk wounded Oxford in the left arm before Oxford then knocked Norfolk's *bevor* off. With the duke's face exposed, Oxford chivalrously declined to continue the combat; however, Norfolk was then struck in the face by an arrow and fell dead at Oxford's feet. This implies that they were fighting on horses, although they were much more likely to be on foot. Beaumont may have taken a degree of artistic licence when describing this and other personal combats, though he does go into extraordinary detail.

Beaumont continues: Lord Surrey, having witnessed his father's death, set out to avenge him, but was stopped and surrounded by superior numbers. Sir Richard Clarendon and Sir William Conyers tried to rescue him but were surrounded by Sir John Savage and his retainers, and cut to pieces. In the meantime, Surrey came face to face with the veteran Sir Gilbert Talbot, who would willingly have spared the life of the young and chivalrous knight. Surrey was wounded but refused to accept quarter, and, when an attempt was made to take him prisoner, killed those who approached him. One last endeavour to capture him was made by a private soldier; Surrey, turning furiously on him, collected his remaining strength and severed the man's arm from his body. The brave earl, worn out with loss of blood, then sank to the earth and presented Talbot with the hilt of his sword, imploring Sir Gilbert to slay him, lest he might die by some ignoble hand. Talbot, on the contrary, spared his life and had him carried from the field.

And where was Northumberland whilst the battle was raging? The *Crowland Chronicle* wrote that:

> In the place where the earl of Northumberland was posted, with a large company of reasonably good men, no engagement could be discerned, and no battle blows given or received.

Molinet also adds:

> The earl of Northumberland ... ought to have charged the French, but did nothing except to flee, both he and his company, to abandon his King Richard, for he had an undertaking with the earl of Richmond, as had some others who deserted him in his need.

Was it his men in the third 'battle' that the chroniclers refer to as traitors? Northumberland was arrested and spent a short period in captivity after the battle, so it is unlikely that he had struck a deal with Henry. It is much more probable that after seeing the French flank attack and the collapse of Norfolk's line, or when Richard

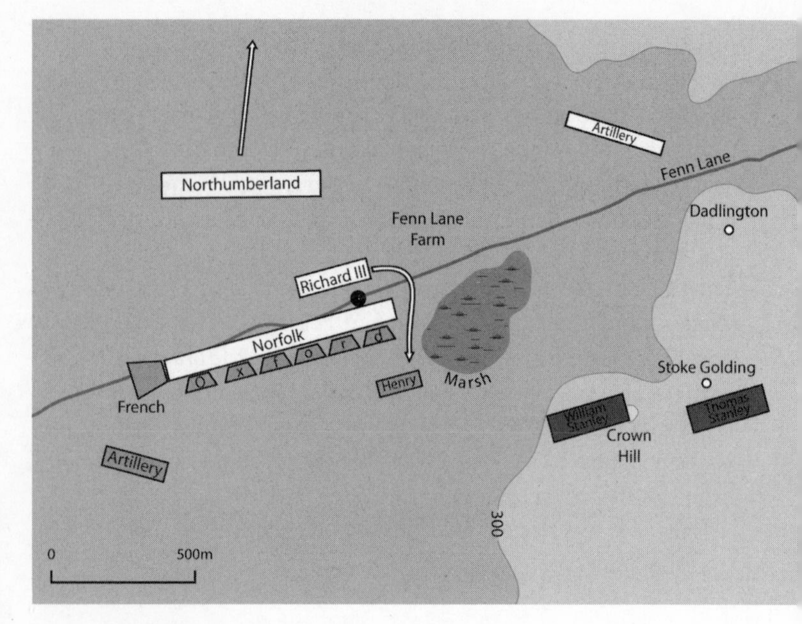


*Fourth phase*

was killed, these raw recruits panicked and ran, deciding that they did not want to suffer the same fate. Molinet reports that the vanguard which was led by the grand chamberlain of England, seeing Richard dead, turned in flight. It was Northumberland, not Norfolk, who was the chamberlain, and one version of the text actually says rearguard, so it is probable that there was an error in translating or transcribing the document at some point.

The situation at this point was dire for Richard, as Norfolk's vanguard was collapsing and Northumberland's men were fleeing. Vergil says that:

> ... king Richard might have sowght to save himself by flight; for they who ever abowt him, seing the soldiers even from the first stroke to lyfc up ther weapons febly and fayntlye, and soome of them to tiepart the feild pryvyly.

This is echoed by *The Ballad of Bosworth Field*, which says:

> ... then to King Richard there came a Knight,
> and said, 'I hold itt time ffor to fflee;
> ffor yonder stanleys dints they be soe wight,
> against them no man may dree'.

*The Song of Lady Bessy* repeats much of *The Ballad of Bosworth Field* except that it claims the knight to be Sir William Harrington. The *Castilian Report* is even more specific, for it says:

> Now when Salaçar, your little vassal, who was there in King Richard's service, saw the treason of the king's people, he went up to him and said: 'Sire, take steps to put your person in safety, without expecting to have the victory in today's battle, owing to the manifest treason in your following.'

The report then says that Richard replied: 'Salazar, God forbid I yield one step. This day I will die as king or win', and with that he put on his coat of arms and his royal crown. The *Castilian Report* says that the crown was worth 120,000 crowns and may have even been the original crown of Edward the Confessor, reputedly destroyed on the orders of Oliver Cromwell after the English Civil War. If it was this crown, then it was too valuable to be worn in battle and it is more likely that he would have worn a simple gold circlet.

By forming his men into wedges Oxford had created gaps in his line, and it was through one of these gaps that Henry's standard was spotted close to the marsh. Richard saw that it was Henry himself with a small body of mounted knights and infantry; if he could just reach Henry and kill him then the battle would be over. Richard gathered his household cavalry and infantry around him and launched the last charge of the Plantagenet dynasty.

*49. The last charge of the Plantagenets. Richard III's fatal charge aimed at Henry and his bodyguards. (Author's collection)*

We do not know which route the charge took, although the ground to the east of the marsh was too boggy and at least one stream would have had to be negotiated, slowing the impetus of any charge to a trot. The deployment of the Stanleys' forces to the east of the marsh must also be taken into account, as they had still not committed to the battle and could have blocked the cavalry before it reached Henry. Speed was of the essence, so they must have taken the shortest route – through the gaps in Oxford's line, west of the marsh. Vergil supports this when he says: 'he strick his horse with the spurres, and runneth owt of thone syde withowt the vanwardes agaynst him.' Beaumont's poem says they charged uphill, which makes sense as behind Henry was placed on the high ground.

Gathering momentum, Richard and his supporters crashed into Henry's bodyguard. Richard killed William Brandon, Henry's standard bearer, and the standard fell to the ground, only to be picked up by a Welshman, Rhys Fawr. Richard's personal standard bearer, Sir Percival Thirwall, was also unhorsed and his legs cut from under him. Henry must have been close because we are told by Vergil that next in Richard's path was:

> … John Cheney a man of muche fortytude, far exceeding the common sort, who encountered with him as he came, but the king with great force drove him to the ground, making way with weapon on every side.

As Henry's men begin to buckle under the weight of the charge, up to 3,000 fresh troops charged down from the hill into Richard's cavalry and infantry, who were still trying to fight their way through to Henry. William Stanley had finally decided to intervene and rescue Henry. Most of Stanley's men, like Richard's men, were probably wearing red surcoats, which must have caused considerable confusion in trying to discern friend from foe as the two sides came to blows.

One by one, Richard's followers were cut down in the melee that followed, before Richard himself was killed. According to Vergil he was 'killyd fyghting manfully in the thickkest presse of his enemyes'. Molinet, on the other hand, writes that 'His horse leapt into a marsh from which it could not retrieve itself. One of the Welshmen then came after him, and struck him dead with a halberd.' In one version of events, it was later claimed that Rhys ap Thomas was the Welshman who killed him, although he was not a halberdier. Another version is that Ralph of Rudyard, which is near Leek in Staffordshire, dealt the fatal blow. Whoever delivered the final *coup de grâce*, Richard III's courage during his last moments was unquestionable, as even his detractors agree. John Rous says that he 'bore himself like a gallant knight and acted with distinction as his own champion until his last breath'. The *Crowland Chronicle* writes that 'King Richard fell in the field, struck by many mortal wounds, as a bold and most valiant prince'. Exactly where Richard died is not known, although a proclamation by Henry soon after the battle says that it was at a place known as 'Sandeford'. Where this was has been lost in time, but it was most likely south of the marsh at a crossing point on one of the streams that fed the marsh. Another fragment of the letter quoted in the Spont paper says that 'he [Henry] wanted to be on foot in the midst of us, and in part we were the reason why the battle was won'. Without the rest of the letter, we do not know in what context this was said; however, it is generally accepted that it implies that Henry retired behind a wall of French pikes when Richard charged. As the French were fighting on the flank, it probably means that Henry simply wanted to be part of the main flanking attack and it was because of this attack that the battle was won.

With Richard's death, any remaining resistance quickly ended; the battle had lasted more than two hours. The cream of the Yorkist nobility was lying dead on the field, including Norfolk, Lord Ferrers, Sir Richard Ratcliffe, Sir Robert Percy, Sir Robert Brackenbury, Sir John Sacheverell and John Kendall. Many of Richard's men threw down their weapons and surrendered or were taken prisoner; those who had not surrendered or had been captured were hunted down like animals as the rout began, with men being hacked down as they fled. There is archaeological evidence to support this in the form of a tail of battlefield debris heading north-east, away from the battle site and

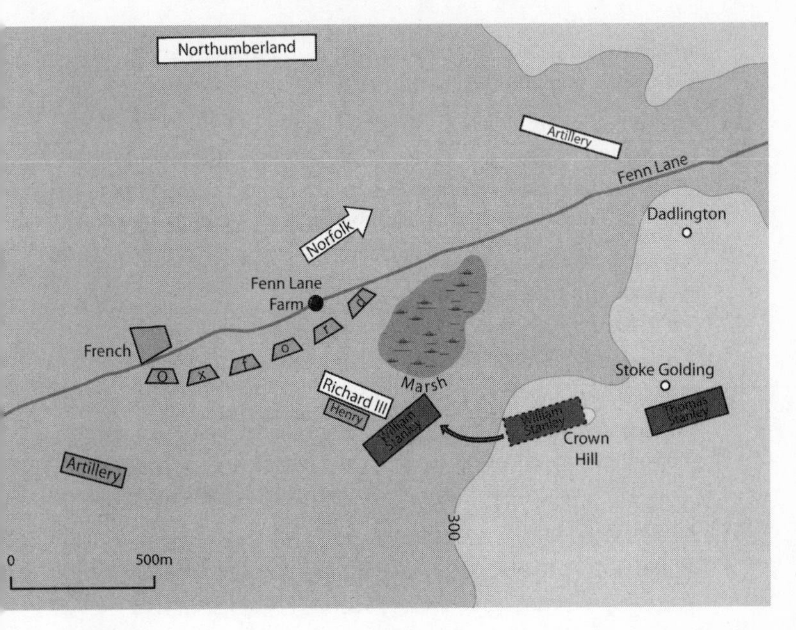


*Fifth phase*

towards Ambion Hill. Some of the fugitives may have reached Daddlington Mill, well over 1km away, as a livery badge of an eagle with wings, probably once owned by a member of John Lord Zouche's household, was recently found close by. It may have been in this area that the remains of the royal army made its last stand and where Zouche was captured. Some, such as Lord Lovell and the Stafford brothers, managed to escape completely and reach sanctuary at St John's in Colchester. Catesby was not so lucky, for he was captured either at the battle or soon after and executed three days later. Significantly, Catesby along with two yeomen, both named Bracher, from the West Country were the only three to be executed after the battle, unlike the bloodbaths that followed the battles during the reign of Edward IV. Perhaps it was because Catesby was Richard's closest advisor and Henry felt he needed to make an example of him. On the other hand, it may have been that Catesby had made too many enemies. In his will, made just after the battle on 25 August, Catesby cryptically asks the Stanleys to 'pray for my soul as ye have not for my body, as I trusted in you'. It reads as if Catesby had surrendered to the Stanleys, who had promised him protection, but then reneged and handed him over for execution. He may have been referring to an earlier deal as well, although exactly what he really meant will probably never be known.

On Henry's side the only notable casualty was William Brandon because, despite Richard's orders, Lord Strange was not executed. *The Song of Lady Bessy* names the man given the task of executing Strange as Latham, but goes on to say that he was stopped by Sir William Harrington. Beaumont's *Ballad of Bosworth Field* disagrees and says that it was Catesby who was given task, but that he was stopped by Lord Ferrers. Was this why the Stanleys handed Catesby over to Henry for execution? Although the *Crowland Chronicle* does not name Strange's saviour, he does say that:

*50. Victorian engraving of Henry being given the crown by Thomas, Lord Stanley. (Author's collection)*

## MEDICINE

If a wounded man survived the day, he would at best be cared for in one of the monastic hospitals. A valued member of a household, on the other hand, would be treated by the lord's surgeon, so he could fight again another day. A recent excavation at the site of the Battle of Towton found the skeleton of a man who had received a horrific cut across the jaw in an earlier battle. However, the wound had been successfully treated before he fell at Towton.

> The persons to whom this duty was entrusted, however, seeing that the issue was doubtful in the extreme, and that a matter of more weight than the destruction of one man was in hand, deferred performance of the king's cruel order, left the man to his own disposal and returned to the thickest of the fight.

We do not know who else died that day, but Vergil puts the numbers of dead as 1,000 men from Richard's army and scarcely 100 from Henry's. Molinet says that only 300 on either side met their demise, whilst the *Castilian Report* gives the total as 10,000. The truth, however, probably lies somewhere in between. With the battle over, the victors looted Richard's baggage train and Richard's royal regalia was collected by Henry's officers and loaded on to his own baggage train. William Stanley was offered the pick of the rest and took a set of Richard's tapestries, which he proudly displayed at one of his residencies, and Henry's mother was sent Richard's personal prayer book.

According to Vergil, with the battle over, Henry gave thanks to God for his victory and withdrew to the nearest hill. From here he thanked his commanders and nobles, knighted Gilbert Talbot, Rhys ap Thomas and Humphrey Stanley, and gave orders that all the dead should be given an honourable burial. Thomas

Stanley then crowned him Henry VII with Richard's own crown, which according to tradition was found under a thorn bush close to where Richard was killed. We do not know how true this story is, although Henry did take the image of a crown and thorn bush as one of his badges soon after. As to the site of this momentous event, part of the high ground behind Henry's battle line, originally known as Garbrody's Hill and Garbrod Field in the fifteenth century, was changed to Crown Hill and Crown Field before 1605, no doubt in reverence to the event.

Richard's body was recovered from the battlefield and, according to Vergil, was 'nakyd of all clothing, and layd uppon an horse bake with the armes and legges hanginge downe on both sides'. The scene was described by the *Crowland Chronicle* as a 'miserable spectacle in good sooth'. His body was then taken back to Leicester. Hall says that he was on the horse of his *Blanc Sanglier Pursuivant*, an officer of arms ranking below a herald but having similar duties, but the *Great Chronicle of London* says that it was a *pursuivant* called Norroy. John Moore was the Norroy King of Arms, a senior herald with jurisdiction north of the River Trent (Nottingham), and his son was at some point *Blanc Sanglier*, so it could have been either. One of the legends associated with the battle says that as Richard rode across Bow Bridge en route to Bosworth, his spur clipped a stone pillar. One of those ubiquitous wise women who witnessed this supposedly announced that where his spur struck, his head would be broken. And sure enough, as Richard's body was carried across the bridge, his head hit the same stone.

# AFTER THE BATTLE

> It is no doubt a good thing to conquer on the field of battle, but it needs greater wisdom and greater skill to make use of victory.
>
> Polybius, *Histories*

Richard's body was put on public display for two days at Greyfriars church, probably in a place of honour. A tomb made of alabaster, with an effigy of Richard on top, was later erected on the orders of Henry. However, the tomb was torn down during the Reformation and whether his remains are still in the church grounds or, as legend has it, thrown into the River Soar, is not known.

Henry also spent two days at Leicester, before sending a proclamation around his new kingdom announcing his accession. With the old administration totally destroyed, Henry had to start again, and it was another month before the business of running the country began in earnest. Sir Robert Willoughby was sent to Sheriff Hutton to arrest Edward, Earl of Warwick, the son of the late Duke of Clarence and last of the male Plantagenets. Willoughby also brought with him Elizabeth, the daughter of Edward IV and Henry's future bride. Elizabeth and her mother were escorted back to London, while the 10-year-old Edward was made a prisoner in the Tower.

Henry made a triumphal entry into London on 3 September, having been met by the mayor and aldermen at Hornsey, who, dressed in all their splendour, escorted him to St Paul's Cathedral. Henry then set about rewarding all those who had helped him: his uncle Jasper was made Duke of Bedford; Philbert de Chandée was made Earl of Bath; Thomas Stanley became Earl of Derby; Edward Courtenay, Earl of Devon; and Sir William Stanley was also given key offices. Henry's official coronation was held on 30 October and eight days later he held his first Parliament.

His first act was to repeal *Titulus Regius*, the statute that declared Edward IV's marriage invalid and his children illegitimate. His second action was to declare himself king from the day before the Battle of Bosworth Field. This meant that anyone who had fought for Richard would be guilty of treason, although, surprisingly, only twenty-eight of Richard's supporters were named in the act of attainder that followed. Richard's nephew and designated heir, John de la Pole, Earl of Lincoln was spared – a decision that Henry would come to regret.

Henry honoured his pledge of December 1483 and married Elizabeth of York on 18 January 1486 at Westminster, uniting the warring houses and giving his children a strong claim to the throne. His heraldic emblem, the Tudor rose, a combination of the white rose of York and the red rose of Lancaster, reflected the unification of the two houses.

Henry's first main concern was how to secure the throne, which he did by dividing and undermining the power of the nobility. His principal weapon was the Court of Star Chamber which revived an earlier practice of using a small group of the Privy Council as a personal or prerogative court, able to cut swiftly through the cumbersome legal system. Serious disputes involving the use of personal power, or threats to royal authority, were dealt with accordingly. Henry allowed the nobles to continue with their regional influence as long as they remained loyal to him.

This, however, was not enough as, less than a year after he was crowned, whilst at Lincoln, Henry became aware of a rebellion by Francis Lovell, Richard's lord chamberlain, along with Humphrey and Thomas Stafford. Together they planned to raise troops and kill Henry as he travelled to the north of England. Henry had them followed, finding the Staffords in Culham church near Abingdon where they were arrested. Sir Richard Edgecombe and Sir William Tyler were sent to arrest Lovell; however, he managed to escape, first joining fellow rebels at Furness Falls and later fleeing to Margaret of York in Flanders. Sir John Conyers, who was also suspected of being involved in the revolt, lost his stewardship of Middleham Castle and had a £2,000 bond imposed.

John de la Pole, Earl of Lincoln, fled to his aunt Margaret, Duchess of Burgundy, at Mechelen (Malines) on 19 March 1487. Here, Margaret provided him with financial and military support in the form of 2,000 German mercenaries, under Martin Schwartz. He was also joined by a number of Yorkist supporters, including Lord Lovell, Sir Richard Harleston, the former governor of Jersey, and Thomas David, a captain of the English garrison at Calais. In April, the army landed in Ireland, claiming that a boy called Lambert Simnel was the Earl of Warwick (who was, in reality, a prisoner in the Tower). On 4 June 1487, de la Pole, his army boosted by a body of Irish troops, crossed over to England. Here they were joined by a number of the local gentry led by Sir Thomas Broughton. In a series of forced marches, the Yorkist army, now numbering some 8,000 men, covered over 320km (200 miles) in five days. On the night of 10 June, at Bramham Moor, outside Tadcaster, Lovell led 2,000 men on a night attack against 400 Lancastrians, led by Lord Clifford. The result was an overwhelming Yorkist victory. On 12 June, de la Pole outmanoeuvred King Henry's northern army, under the command of the Earl of Northumberland, by ordering a force under John, Lord Scrope, to mount a diversionary attack on Bootham Bar in York. Lord Scrope then withdrew northwards, taking Northumberland's army with him.

De la Pole and the main army continued south. They met with a body of Lancastrian cavalry under Lord Scales outside Doncaster, and three days of skirmishing through Sherwood Forest followed. Eventually, Scales was forced to retreat to Nottingham; however, the fighting allowed Henry time to bring up substantial reinforcements under the command of Lord Strange, who arrived at Nottingham on 14 June. The next day they began moving north-east toward Newark after receiving news that Lincoln had crossed the River Trent. At around 9 a.m. on 16 June, Henry's vanguard, commanded by the Earl of Oxford, encountered the Yorkist army on the brow of a hill by the River Trent at the village of East Stoke. The Yorkists were surrounded on three sides and attacked immediately. However, the unarmoured Irish were cut to pieces and the German mercenaries, unable to retreat, fought to the last man. The battle lasted for three hours and de la Pole, Fitzgerald, Broughton and Schwartz were all killed in the fighting. Only Lord Lovell escaped and, according to legend, died hidden in a secret room at his house, while Simnel was captured and made a servant in the royal kitchen by Henry. Twenty-eight Yorkists were attained in the aftermath, but the Irish were pardoned. Following the death of his older brother John, Edmund de la Pole became the leading Yorkist claimant to the throne. Henry allowed him to succeed as Duke of Suffolk in 1491, although some time later Edmund's title was demoted to the rank of earl.

Three years later a man appeared claiming to be Richard, the younger of the Princes in the Tower. Known as Perkin Warbeck, he won the support of Edward IV's sister Margaret of Burgundy and in 1491 landed in Ireland, but found little support. Returning to the European mainland, he was first received by Charles VIII of France, but was expelled in 1492 under the terms of the Treaty of Etaples, in which Charles had agreed not to shelter rebels against the Tudors. However, the Duke of York, as Warbeck became known, was rapidly gaining popular support across Europe and was proving to be an embarrassment to Henry. Warbeck was even recognised as King Richard IV of England by the Holy Roman Emperor, Maximilian I. England began to fracture again, with many Yorkist supporters re-emerging in the belief that Warbeck was to be the heir to the Yorkist dynasty. Others, discontent with Henry's rule, joined them. Henry sent spies to Margaret of Burgundy in Flanders, claiming to be Yorkist supporters. Here they discovered the names of many of the conspirators, who were promptly arrested and charged with treason. The list included Lord Fitzwalter, Sir Simon Mountford, William Daubeney and Robert Ratcliffe, as well as a number of priests. Significantly, the list also included Sir William Stanley, who had helped Henry to the throne in the first place. William was beheaded on 10 July 1495.

On 3 July 1495, funded by Margaret of Burgundy, Warbeck landed at Deal in Kent, but his small army was routed and 150 of his men were killed before he even disembarked. He was forced to return to Ireland, where, finding support from the Earl of Desmond, he laid siege to Waterford. In the face of fierce resistance, he later fled to Scotland where he received support from the king, James IV. An army was raised, crossing the River Tweed at Coldstream on 19 September 1496. They were at Hetoune (Castle Heaton) on 24 September, where miners demolished four towers. An English army under Lord Neville advanced from Newcastle to meet them and, with dwindling supplies, Warbeck's army returned home. After signing a peace treaty with England, James sent Warbeck back to Ireland where he once again laid siege to Waterford. This time four English ships chased him away after only eleven days.

At the beginning of 1497, another rebellion was fomenting in Cornwall, this time over heavy taxation. Michael Joseph (also known as An Gof – the smith), a blacksmith from St Keverne, and Thomas Flamank, a lawyer of Bodmin, incited many of the people of Cornwall into armed revolt against the king. An army of 15,000 gathered at Bodmin and marched into Devon, and from there they headed for Kent where they hoped to gain additional support. They were joined en route by James Touchet, Baron Audley, who acted as a 'political' leader.

After being rebuffed by the men of Kent the army marched on London, arriving at Guildford on 13 June. The royal family had moved to the Tower of London for safety, whilst in the rest of the city there was a feeling of panic. It was said that there was a general cry of 'Every man to harness! To harness!' as citizens armed themselves, lining the walls and gates. Meanwhile, Henry sent an army of 8,000 men under Giles, Lord Daubeney, to Hounslow Heath. Lord Daubeney sent out a force of 500 mounted spearmen and they clashed with the Cornish at 'Gill Down' outside Guildford on 14 June. The Cornish army marched to Blackheath, but by this time many had returned home and only 9,000–10,000 remained.

Meanwhile, Henry had been assembling an army of over 25,000 men to counter the threat and, after carefully spreading rumours that he would attack on the following Monday, Henry moved against the Cornish at dawn on Saturday 17 June 1497. Lacking cavalry and artillery, the Cornish placed a body of archers at the bridge at Deptford Strand, with the rest of the army near to the top of the hill on Blackheath. Two of the three royal 'battles' under Lords Oxford, Essex and Suffolk wheeled round the right flank and to the rear of the Cornishmen. Once the Cornish were surrounded, Lord Daubeney and the third 'battle' were ordered into frontal attack. A group of spearmen under Sir Humphrey Stanley moved forward, breaking through the Cornish archers, while Lord Daubeney and his men poured across the bridge and engaged the Cornish head on. The two other 'battles' then attacked and the Cornish army was cut in pieces. Estimates of the Cornish dead range from 200 to 2,000 and a general slaughter of the broken army was well under way when An Gof gave the order to surrender. An Gof, Audley and Flamank were all captured and executed. As punishment, Crown agents extracted severe monetary penalties against the county, which caused some parts to be impoverished for many years to come.

On 7 September 1497, hoping to capitalise on the Cornish people's resentment in the aftermath of their uprising, Warbeck landed at Whitesand Bay, near Land's End, in Cornwall. He proclaimed that he would put a stop to extortionate taxes levied to help fight a war against Scotland and was warmly welcomed. He was declared 'Richard IV' on Bodmin Moor and his Cornish army of some 3,000 strong marched on Exeter, where they were twice beaten off. Lord Daubeney was again sent to deal with the rebellion, but when Warbeck heard that scouts were at Glastonbury he panicked and fled to sanctuary in Beaulieu Abbey in Hampshire. Warbeck eventually surrendered and was imprisoned, first at Taunton and then the Tower. Henry reached Taunton on 4 October 1497, where he received the surrender of the remaining Cornish army; the ringleaders were executed and others fined.

Warbeck was held in the Tower alongside Edward, Earl of Warwick, and it appears that the two tried to escape at some point during 1499. In his confession, possibly obtained under torture, Warbeck said he was Flemish and born to a man called John Osbeck (also known as Jehan de Werbecque) in Tournai. In 1491, aged about 17, he was taken to Cork in Ireland where he learnt to speak English. He then claimed that upon seeing him dressed in silk clothes, some of the Yorkist citizens of Cork demanded to '[do] him the honour as a member of the Royal House of York'. He said they did this because they were resolved in gaining revenge on the King of England and decided that he would claim to be the younger son of King Edward IV. Despite the confession, his true identity is still a mystery and a number of historians have suggested that his story was to try to avoid execution. However, on 23 November 1499, he was drawn on a hurdle from the Tower to Tyburn and was hanged as a commoner after reading out the confession. Five days later Edward was beheaded, allegedly for treason.

Not all of Richard's supporters stayed loyal to the Yorkist cause, however. Thomas Howard, Earl of Surrey, spent three years in prison after Bosworth, but eventually was restored to the earldom. In 1499 he was recalled to court and accompanied the king on a state visit to France in the following year. Surrey was an executor of the will of King Henry VII and played a prominent role in the coronation of King Henry VIII, in which he served as earl marshal. He would also go on to command the English army at the Battle of Flodden, crushing a much larger Scottish army, and on 1 February 1514 was created Duke of Norfolk. Meanwhile, Edmund de la Pole, who was now the Yorkist heir, had fled England in 1501 with the aid of Sir James Tyrrell, seeking the help of Maximilian I. In 1506, Maximilian's son, Phillip of Burgundy, was blown off course while sailing to Castile and unexpectedly became a guest of Henry VII. Whilst in England, Phillip was persuaded to hand Edmund over to Henry on the proviso that he would not be harmed.

On 21 April 1509, Henry died of tuberculosis at Richmond Palace and was buried at Westminster Abbey. His second son, Henry VIII, succeeded him and ruled for the next forty-five years. There remained a Yorkist party within the court led by Lady Salisbury, Margaret Pole, daughter of the Duke of Clarence, and Henry Courtenay, Marquis of Exeter. The marquis was the son of Catherine, the youngest daughter of Edward IV, and therefore heir to the throne after the Tudors. Like his father, Henry VIII was plagued with rebellion, but he was not so forgiving and would eventually eradicate the Yorkist line. In 1513 he had Edmund de la Pole executed. His younger brother, Richard, declared himself Earl of Suffolk soon after and remained the leading Yorkist claimant until his death at the Battle of Pavia on 24 February 1525. However, the biggest threat to Henry's rule came in 1536, when 9,000 men marched on London. It was known as the 'Pilgrimage of Grace' and was essentially a protest against the political and economic situation.

In 1538, Henry Courtenay was accused of a plot to depose Henry. He was arrested and then executed by decapitation with a sword on Tower Hill on 9 January 1539. Margaret Pole was also arrested for her alleged involvement in the plot and on the morning of 27 May 1541, aged 68, she was executed at the Tower of London on Henry's orders. Frail and ill, she refused to lay her head on the block and, as she struggled, the inexperienced executioner's first blow made a gash in her shoulder rather than her neck. It took ten more blows to complete the execution and, with the final blow, the Plantagenets were no more.

# THE LEGACY

## Bosworth as a Tudor Victory

The so called 'Renaissance' had already started when Henry claimed the throne as William Caxton had begun to publish books under the patronage of Lord Rivers, Sir Anthony Woodville and then Richard III. An act of 1484, under Richard III, had specifically exempted 'merchant strangers' from any restrictions on either printing in England or bringing in books from abroad, introducing new ideas and ideals. After Richard's death, Margaret Beaufort became his main patron and in 1490 he printed the statutes of the first three parliaments of Henry VII, the first time the statutes of England were produced in English rather than legal French.

Henry VII's descendants would be responsible for radical changes in England. Besides being remembered for his six marriages, his son, Henry VIII (1491–1547), was instrumental in the separation of the Church of England from the Roman Catholic Church, and the 'Dissolution of the Monasteries'. Henry VII's granddaughter, Queen Elizabeth I (1558–1603) ushered in a period now known as the 'Golden Age', which was a time of national pride through classical ideals and international

*51. Richard III's badge and motto in stained glass at York Minster. (Author's collection)*

## THE ENGLISH LANGUAGE

When the wars started, English had only been universally spoken by the aristocracy for around fifty years. Before then French was their main language, and this is why today many of the words that are related to those pursuits that were once restricted to the aristocracy, such as politics, law and war, have French origins.

expansion. It was an age of exploration and expansion abroad and the height of the so-called 'English Renaissance', which saw the flowering of poetry, music, literature and the theatre of William Shakespeare.

On Elizabeth's death, James VI of Scotland (1566–1625) succeeded to the English throne as James I, joining the two countries for the first time. It was also the time of the 'Gunpowder Plot', which was led by Robert Catesby, a descendant of William Catesby, Richard III's right-hand man. Throughout the Tudor age, plots, conspiracies and rebellions continued to haunt its rulers, although the Protestant/Catholic divide was often at its heart. After Bosworth, all the kings and queens still believed in the right of divine rule and, although Parliament grew in power during the period, it was not strong enough to challenge the ruler; it would be 157 years before it could do that and would lead to another bloody civil war.

## Bosworth's Place in History

Sir Thomas More, a leading councillor of Henry VIII, wrote *The History of King Richard III*, which was the first literary work to portray Richard as a vile monster and is believed to have been heavily influenced by John Morton, More's mentor and one of the main conspirators in the rebellions against Richard. Whilst it lacks historical accuracy, it is however noted for its literary skill and adherence to classical principles; Shakespeare would go on to write his play *Richard III* largely based on More's work and would blacken Richard's character completely. Since then there have been many books written about Richard and also the fate of the Princes in the Tower, with some generally agreeing with More, while others believe that Richard was a good king and a victim of Tudor propaganda.

It was William Hutton who wrote the first detailed study of the battle, *The Battle of Bosworth-Field,* in 1788. He placed the location of the battle as Ambion Hill, largely based on a comment by Polydore Vergil that: 'King Richard pitched his field on a hill called Anne Beame, refreshed his souldiers and took his rest.' For many years to come this would be the accepted site.

In 1974 Leicestershire County Council, with the agreement and co-operation of the local farmers and landowners, set up

*52. Richard's livery badge. One similar to this was found on the site of the battle. (Author's collection)*

a visitor centre at Ambion Hill Farm. However, during the years that followed, several historians put forward alternative locations for the battle and all have their merits, making it increasingly probable that Ambion Hill was not the actual site of the battle. In 2005, Leicestershire County Council commissioned the Battlefields Trust to find the exact location of the battlefield, and a team of specialists from many different disciplines were brought together to carry out the search. They finally found the site almost 3km (1.8 miles) from Ambion Hill, after a metal detector survey covering 7sq km. The survey discovered a concentration of over thirty-two pieces of lead shot, some from hand-guns and others, up to 93mm in diameter, from field artillery pieces of the time. Although the first major use of artillery in the wars was at the Battle of Northampton in 1460, more shot was found at this one site than all those previously found on all the medieval battlefields of Europe put together. Another key find was a 30mm-long, silver-gilt livery badge of a boar, close to the edge of an area that was once marsh. This was King Richard III's own personal badge and would almost certainly have been worn and lost by a knight of King Richard's retinue in the heat of battle, probably during Richard's last charge. On 19 February 2010, the real location of the battle was finally revealed to the public.

# ORDERS OF BATTLE

## The Royal Army

Overall Commander: Richard Plantagenet, King Richard III

### The Vanward

Commander: John Howard, 1st Duke of Norfolk
Thomas Howard, Earl of Surrey

### The Mainward

Commander: Richard Plantagenet, King Richard III
Standard bearer: Sir Percival Thirwall

### The Rearward

Commander: Henry Percy, Earl of Northumberland
Commissions of array
Northampton (Sir Roger Wake)
Coventry

## Henry Tudor's Army

Overall Commander: Henry Tudor, Earl of Richmond

### The Vanward

Commander: John de Vere, Earl of Oxford
Right flank: Gilbert Talbot
Left flank: Sir John Savage

### Henry Tudor's bodyguard

Jasper Tudor, Earl of Pembroke
Sir John Cheyne of Falstone Cheney
Standard bearer, Sir William Brandon of Soham

### French Mercenaries

Commander: Philibert de Chandée of Brittany

### Scottish Mercenaries

Cavalry, Alexander Bruce
Infantry, John of Haddington

# FURTHER READING

## Sources

Doutrepont, G. and O. Jodogne (eds), *Chroniques de Jean Molinet (1474–1506)*, 3 vols (1935–37)

Dupont, L.M.E. (ed.), *Memoirs of Philippe de Commines* (1840)

Hall, Edward, *The Union of the Two Noble Families of Lancaster and York*

Mancini, Dominic, *The Usurpation of Richard III*, edited and translated by C.A.J. Armstrong (Sutton, 1984)

Nokes, E.M. and G. Wheeler (trans), *A Castilian Report,* in 'A Spanish account of the battle of Bosworth', in *The Ricardian,* 2, no. 36 (1972)

'Parliamentary record, "Act of Attainder", November 1485"', in *Rotuli Parliamentorum,* Vol. VI, edited by J. Strachey (1767–83)

'Proclamation of Henry Tudor, 22–23 August, 1485', in *Tudor Royal Proclamations,* Vol. I, 'The Early Tudors', edited by P.L. Hughes and J.P. Larkin (1964)

Pronay, N. & J. Cox (eds), *The Crowland Chronicle Continuations, 1459–1486* (London, 1986)

Rous of Warwick, John, *Historia Johannis Rossi Warwicensis de Regibus Anglie*, edited by T. Hearne (1716)

Thomas, A.H. and I.D. Thornley (eds), *The Great Chronicle of London* (George W. Jones, 1938)
Vergil, Polydore, *The Anglica Historia of Polydore Vergil*, edited and translated by D. Hay, Camden Soc., 3rd ser., 74 (1950)

All the original texts can be found on the American branch of the Richard III Society website (http://www.r3.org)

## The Battle

Bennett, M.J., *The Battle of Bosworth* (Sutton, 2000)
English Heritage, 'Battlefield Report: Bosworth 1485' (1995)
Foard. G., 'Discovering Bosworth', in *British Archaeology* (May/June 2010)
Foss, P., *The Field of Redemore: The Battle of Bosworth, 1485* (Rosalba Press, 1990)
Hammond, P., *Richard III and the Bosworth Campaign* (Pen and Sword, 2010)
Hammond, P.W. and A. Sutton, *Richard III: The Road to Bosworth Field* (Constable, 1985)
Jones, M.K., *Bosworth 1485: Psychology of a Battle* (Tempus, 2002)

## Richard III and Henry VII

Carson, A., *Richard III: Maligned King* (The History Press; Reprint edition, 2009)
Chrimes, S.B., *Henry VII* (Methuen, 1972)
Dockray, K., *Richard III: A Source Book* (Sutton, 1997)
Gill, L., *Richard III and Buckingham's Rebellion* (Sutton, 2000)
Hicks, M., *Richard the Third* (Tempus, 2001)
Kendall, P.M. (ed.), *Richard III: The Great Debate* (W.W. Norton, 1992)
Kendall, P.M., *Richard the Third* (W.W. Norton, 1956)

Penn, T., *Winter King: The Dawn of Tudor England* (Allen Lane, 2011)
Pollard, A.J., *Richard III and the Princes in the Tower* (St Martin's Press, 1991)
Ross, C., *Good King Richard III* (Methuen, 1981)

## The Wars of the Roses

Haigh, P., *Military Campaigns of the Wars of the Roses* (Sutton, 1995)
Hicks, M., *The Wars of the Roses 1455–1485* (Osprey Publishing, 2003)
Lander, J.R., *The Wars of the Roses* (Sutton, 1990)
Pollard, A.J., *The Wars of the Roses* (MacMillan Education Ltd, 1988)
Ross, C., *The Wars of the Roses: A Concise History* (Thames and Hudson, 1976)
Royale, T., *The Wars of the Roses* (Abacus, 2010)

## Military Aspects

Boardman, A.W., *The Medieval Soldier in the Wars of the Roses* (Sutton, 1998)
Goodman, A., *The Wars of the Roses: Military Activity and English Society, 1452–97* (Routledge, 1990)
Goodman, A., *The Wars of the Roses: The Soldiers' Experience* (The History Press, 2006)
McGill, P. and J. Jones, *Standards, Badges & Livery Colours of the Wars of the Roses* (Freezywater Publishing, 1992)
Pizan, C. and C. Cannon Willard (tr.), S. Willard (ed.), *The Book of Deeds of Arms and of Chivalry* (Penn State Press, 1999)
Strickland, M. and R. Hardy, *The Great Warbow* (Haynes Publishing, 2011)

## Websites

The Richard III Society: http://www.richardiii.net
American branch of the Richard III Society is a useful resource for all things related to the Wars of the Roses: http://www.r3.org
Richard III Foundation. Each year the organisation hosts a conference on Bosworth related topics: http://richard111.com

## Places to Visit

A visit to the Bosworth Battlefield Visitor Centre is a must for anyone interested in the period. Sited on Ambion Hill, and with something for all ages, there is a large exhibition of the battle, with interactive maps, displays of weapons and equipment etc., and also battlefield walks and regular tours of the area, a gift shop and restaurant. On the anniversary of the battle, the centre holds the Bosworth Festival, which includes re-enactments of the battle. For more details, see http://www.bosworthbattlefield.com

## Re-enacting

There are many groups all over the UK who perform re-enactments of the Wars of the Roses period. Most come under two umbrella organisations: The Wars of the Roses Federation at http://www.et-tu.com/wotrf1/cgi-bin/index.cgi and The Medieval Siege Society at http://www.medieval-siege-society.co.uk

## Wargaming

For those who wish to wargame the period, figures can be brought in all scales. Some of the best 28mm are Perry Miniatures (http://www.perry-miniatures.com), who manufacture both plastic and metal, and Front Rank Figurines (http://www.frontrank.com), who manufacture in metal only. Peter Pig (http://www.peterpig.co.uk)

produce an excellent range in 15mm, as does Baccus (http://www.baccus6mm.com) in 6mm. There are also growing number of rule sets available including *Field of Glory* (Osprey), *Hail Caesar* (Warlord Games) and *Clash of Empires* (Great Escape Games). Flags for the period can be brought from Freezywater Publications amongst others.

# INDEX